WAYFARERS
IN THE COSMOS

GEORGE V. COYNE, S.J.

AND

ALESSANDRO OMIZZOLO

VATICAN OBSERVATORY

WAYFARERS
IN THE COSMOS

THE HUMAN QUEST
FOR MEANING

A Crossroad Book
The Crossroad Publishing Company
New York

The Crossroad Publishing Company
481 Eighth Avenue, New York, NY 10001

Printed in the United States of America

Library of Congress Cataloging-in-Publication Data

Coyne, G. V.
   Wayfarers in the cosmos : the human quest for meaning /
George V. Coyne and Alessandro Omizzolo.
     p. cm.
   Includes bibliographical references.
   ISBN 0-8245-1912-4 (hardcover)
   1. Cosmology. 2. Religion and science. 3. Catholic
Church–Doctrines. I. Omizzolo, Alessandro. II. Title.
BX1795.S35 C69 2002
291.2′4–dc21

                  2001006099

1 2 3 4 5 6 7 8 9 10   08 07 06 05 04 03 02

CONTENTS

v

103441

WAYFARERS
IN THE COSMOS

INTRODUCTION

WHEN WE HUMAN BEINGS think about ourselves in comparison with all else we experience in the universe, we recognize that we have much in common and yet that we are different. More than any other creatures we know we sense that we are open to an immense and rich array of possibilities in the way we exist and in the way we lead our lives. This is, perhaps, best described by saying that we are symbolic creatures. Like symbols we are always leaning toward a reality beyond ourselves. We are never fully content with what we are now. We are directed to the other and to the future. Our very physical makeup, the constant tension in our flesh toward growth or toward disintegration, hints at this. Our need to love and to be loved, our unquenchable thirst to understand and to manage the environment in which we live, all speak to this.

Among the many symbolic actions which express the nature of us humans one of the most meaningful and at the same time simple ones is perhaps our gaze toward the sky in search of familiarity and understanding. That gesture of raising one's head and lifting one's eyes to gaze beyond immediate realities does not express so much a disorientation as it does an acknowledgement of insufficiency, of the need for something or someone out there, beyond oneself. Ancient mythologies, cosmologies, and cosmogonies bear witness to the immense power which drives us humans in our continuous search for deeper understanding. Modern science bears witness to this persistent journey. From time immemorial we have always sought this further understanding in a person with whom we could converse, someone who shared our capacity to love and be loved and our desire to understand and to accomplish something of significance.

The opening scene of the film *2001: A Space Odyssey* expresses this very well. When that human-like ape tosses up the bone of his rival whom he has just killed and begins to follow closely its path across the sky, he becomes in that instant human. The symbolism is evident. The killing of that which is pure animality opens the one-time killer to a new existence and a new view of things, a view which looks on high toward the heavens. It is one way of acting out the statement of Camus:

> The whole earth is designed in such a way
> that the face may turn upward
> and the gaze may begin to explore

Our attempts, therefore, to understand the universe have as much to say about ourselves as they do about the universe. In fact, in us the universe can reflect upon itself, and from our reflections there grows the conviction that we are part of that upon which we are reflecting. As soon as we set out with the powerful instruments of mathematics and physics to understand the universe and our place in it, we are made aware that we are standing on the shoulders of giants and that the path which has led to what we know today has been, with respect to a human lifetime, a long and arduous one and that many have gone before us. But, in comparison to the age of the universe, it has really been quite a short trek.

It makes us dizzy to contemplate the billions of years that the universe has been evolving and then to think that we are on a little planet orbiting a quite normal star, one of the 200 billion stars in the Milky Way. And then we realize that the Milky Way is just one galaxy and not anything special among the billions of galaxies which populate the visible universe.

We invite the reader to join us wayfarers as we retrace the most important of the steps taken on this journey of understanding and as we reflect upon the journey itself in order to appreciate where we are today on our continuing voyage in a universe ever grander and more mysterious. Our journey is a twofold one. We will take a trip through history to see how various cultures and civilizations have contributed to our scientific knowledge of the universe. Certain key personages will stand out as milestones on that journey. We will also take a trip along the path of the key scientific discoveries which have with time contributed to our knowledge of the universe. Our goal is to share with the reader our experiences both as scientists and as religious believers as we continue this twofold journey.

We will discover how ancient civilizations, in particular, the Egyptians, the Assyrians, the Babylonians, and the Greeks, observed the heavens and how they made use of their data (chapter 1). Very soon afterward the heavens became a subject of philosophical considerations, and

it was in ancient Greece that these tendencies matured
(chapter 2) and established a basis for the birth of science. Such studies grew with the establishment of the
first universities and this in turn led to the rediscovery of
ancient manuscripts. All of this nourished the desire for a
deeper understanding of nature, even though this would
lead to challenges against theories which until then were
indisputable (chapter 3). Some of the great figures of
Western culture are of particular interest because they
made important contributions to science and, in particular, to astronomy. We speak of them in chapters 4, 5,
and 6. These giants of science bring us to the threshold
of our own epoch, to the new visions of the universe
to which we have come through further research upon
their discoveries and to an appreciation of the difficulties
which they encountered. Thus we come to look upon the
stars in a new light and to unveil the mysteries they once
held (chapter 7), and then we journey further into a universe grander than anything our ancestors could have
imagined (chapter 8).

The vastness and the richness of modern scientific discoveries have drawn us into a whole array of questions,
some old, some new, and not only scientific ones, which
we will try to gather together into a summary as a prepa-
ration for a journey which, as best we can judge, seems
to be only beginning. While, in fact, we seem to be approaching our goal, we realize at the end that it appears
to be unreachable and that perhaps for that very reason it always fascinates us and draws us on to further
adventures (chapter 9).

We have no doubt that science has been a dominating

influence in setting the direction of our journey. Nevertheless, we have become aware, in our attempt to unify our scientific knowledge with all that we have come to experience as human beings, that there is much in our experience that lies outside the domain of science. We experience a passionate desire to understand, and we sense that it is a call to Love. Science, it is important to note, has brought us to this, a science which today, more than ever in the past, throws open the doors to realities before which it senses that it is not totally competent, realities which require different approaches from those with which science itself is familiar. Science today is ever more human; it stimulates, provokes, questions us in ways that drive us beyond science in the search for satisfaction, while at the same time scientific data furnish the stimuli. In this context the best science, to its great merit, does not pretend nor presume to have the ultimate answers. It simply suggests and urges us on, well aware that not all is within its ken. Freedom to seek further understanding, and not a dogmatic possession of that which is partially understood, characterizes the best scientists. Science, in fact, is a field where certainties lie always in the future; thus science is vital, dynamic, and very demanding of those who seek to discover the secrets of the universe.

In this book the reader will find an attempt to read the data of science more from a human than a scientific perspective, without any presupposition, however, that the one precludes the other. In fact, it is an altogether very human endeavor to attempt to integrate rigorous scientific conclusions with those drawn from life's other experiences and from the very search for the meaning of life. And since we the authors are also believers we cannot do other than bring this faith dimension into our view of the heavens in our search to uncover its mysteries. As believers, however, we have no illusion that by faith we automatically possess the truth; quite the contrary, we are very aware that the truth is not to be possessed but to be contemplated. Contemplation is an end in itself, and the object contemplated serves no other end than to bring the joy of contemplation to the observer. In this sense it is our wish that this work bear witness to the fact that the search for truth brings with it many ways of knowing in addition to the commonly accepted ones. The truth itself requires that we neither exclude nor absolutize any possibility, if for no other reason than that our search be complete. In so doing we sense that we are entering more profoundly into Love and allowing ourselves to be taught and caught by it.

Chapter One

OUR FIRST STEPS,
OUR ANCESTORS

THE WORD which was customarily used by our ancestors, and is now used by us moderns, to designate
the unity of everything we see in the heavens is "cosmos." It is perhaps worth remembering that the original
meaning of "cosmos" in ancient Greek was "order, harmony." Its use, therefore, to describe the heavens meant
that one saw in the heavens a certain harmonious order,
an aesthetical dimension in the ordering. The heavens
appeared as beautiful, as something which at first sight
gave rise to the kinds of emotional experiences which
always surge forth from that which appears beautiful
spontaneously: experiences of amazement, admiration,
joy, gratitude. But alongside this way of thinking there
was another, a perhaps more dominant one. Although
harmonious, the heavens were also dominated by a sense
of the unknown. And while the unknown always gives
rise to a sense of admiration and of curiosity, it also
gives rise to fear. It was with this ambivalent feeling that
our ancestors approached the heavens. The heavens were
harmonious but also frightening.

We have come to this understanding of "cosmos,"

which is not just a matter of words but also a way of thinking, after a long intellectual journey which carried us, at least those of us in the West, through the civilizations which preceded the Greeks. That historical journey is a shared archetype for the continuous wandering of each one of us as we search within ourselves and about us for answers to the questions which the universe puts to us. It is precisely because we are human beings that we sense an urgency to respond, or at least to seek to respond as best we can, to these questions. A kind of healthy uneasiness characterizes this journey, and it drives each of us to ever new havens. We might synthesize these havens in a single word, "cosmos," a word, which, like a jewel box, contains the collective results of an unwavering intellectual search which longs to obtain a deeper understanding of ourselves in the universe. We are like wayfarers who set out knowing that we must rely upon ourselves, upon our own physical strength and intellectual prowess.

The idea of cosmos is one of the precious fruits gathered from the diligent use of the capacity we humans have to organize our thoughts by relying upon both reason and logic. In antiquity at the dawn of knowledge human beings unified their various experiences of themselves and the universe in the use of the term "cosmos."

We are now going to take a kind of voyage into the past, a journey to the source of all journeying to try to understand how we have come to this weighty concept of "cosmos." As we do so, we are convinced that we will find from the past useful hints for our journey into the future as we in turn are driven by the same insatiable desire to know which brought about the wise insights of our ancestors. To regain that wisdom may be the only motive which can give meaning to us humans of the third millennium who, although with technologies enormously more advanced than those of thousands of years ago, can make the best use of them only by going back to that which has served so well in the past: intelligence and the love of learning.

As we look back at our ancestors we realize that one of the first goals of their journey was to see the heavens, their lives, nature, and all that was happening to them as a gift from on high. Their gods took care of everything. They created, protected, and sustained the cosmos, including life. In fact, the cosmos was a stage on which the human adventure was acted out. It could, at the command of the gods, take on at one time the aspect of a tragedy and at another that of a comedy. The birth, growth, decline, and death of the human being, as well as the sequence of the seasons, of day and night, of the rising, the passage, and the setting of the stars, of the maturing of the crops, all had only one explanation, and that lay in the existence and presence of the gods who determined everything. Then there was the sky at the same time so clear and yet so dark that one could not help but be moved by admiration and wonder for its beauty, worthy of the one who had made it. The heavens were not only the work of the gods; it was where they lived. So thought the Sumerians, Babylonians, Assyrians, Egyptians, Greeks, Romans, Incas, Aztecs, Mayans, Chinese, Indians, etc. The sky was the home of the gods, and only a few, especially fortunate, humans could hope, upon dying, to live there.

The relationship between creators and the created varied according to the civilizations and the epoch under consideration. Thus we witness an evolution in the way that human beings think about the cosmos and about the gods and about the relationship of the cosmos to the gods and to themselves. While, for example, the Egyptians have their gods dwelling in the universe under the form of stars, or of animals, or of rivers, we begin with the reflections of the Greeks to see already a progressive separation of the divine from the world. There appears to be a desire to insinuate a sharp separation between that which is corruptible (the created) and that which is not (the gods). The creation myths which arose in these various civilizations tell us of these diverse ideas. Creation will be seen as an action which involves a principal god and a series of minor gods who assume the role of intermediary between the principal god and the worlds. These minor gods do not have the same prerogatives or perfections which the principal god or gods possess, so they serve to establish the distinction between the imperfection of the created world and the purity of the realm of the gods.

However, it is necessary in this regard to distinguish between what the common person believed and what those who were professionally dedicated to reflecting upon these matters thought. This distinction is important because it will have something to do with the separation which, with time, will increase between the scientific viewpoint and that of the common person. This separation has been detrimental to both science and society at large, and it threatens to continue to be so. As time has gone by, false ideas about science have arisen and become fixed in the mind of the public precisely because of an increasing lack of knowledge by the public of scientific results. Thus society is deprived of that knowledge of nature which is part of our cultural heritage and to which every person has a right. Increasing specialization in scientific research, accompanied by a language limited to those involved in the research, adds a further obstacle to the exchange of knowledge. This not only deprives us of information, but it also makes it increasingly difficult to fulfill our desire to come to an ever more complete synthesis of what we know.

This desire for a synthesis of our knowledge will, however, also bring us through philosophical reflection to evaluate the place of the human being within creation. That place will for many centuries assume a supremely important centrality, as can be seen in all of the geocentric models of the cosmos. Thus humans acquired for themselves something of the divine. In this regard, one of the biblical accounts of creation is significant. It places man as the last act of creation; all else was made for him and he is at the center of the cosmos.

One thing is certain among all of the ancient concepts of the cosmos: the observation of the sky becomes a "cultural" experience or expresses "culture," in the sense that it determines social, religious, political, and economic relationships. One must look to the sky to extract information on the fate of individuals and nations, to obtain hints as to what direction to take in political and strategic decisions, to know when to sow and when to reap, to predict the weather, to know the outcome of a conflict. Everything is ruled by the heavens. This is a kind of universal cosmic religion whose echoes reverberate even to our own day. In fact, one can still hear it said that not a leaf flutters unless God wills it. This attitude translates into religious worship which expresses itself in rites of propitiation for fertility, for rain, and for whatever else makes life more liveable. The priestly caste obviously presided over these rites. The priests, however, were also, and not by chance, the scientists. The one who scanned the heavens to understand the designs of the gods, the one who snatched secrets from the gods, might also be the same one who knew the secrets of nature. It is not surprising, therefore, that the first solar and lunar calendars are drawn up precisely within the context of religious worship. Duly translated these calendars will become the only means for the farmer to calculate when to sow and when to reap.

The pleasure of confronting the unknown and revealing its secrets very soon drove early humans to navigate rivers and the sea. While movements on the earth were fairly easy, since one had fixed reference points in certain rock formations, mountains, rivers, etc., things were more complicated on water when the coastline and thus fixed reference points disappeared from view. So, rock formations, mountains, and rivers are replaced by the vault of the heavens as the reference background for secure travel without fear of getting lost. But it was always the gods who watched over the voyages and the stars, which often represented the gods and assured their presence. To get to where one was going required that one not only worship the gods in heaven but also have a technical knowledge of the heavens. One had to know where and when the sun and the moon rose and set, how the planets and the stars moved, how to identify the constellations. All of this was essential to the seafarer.

Thus, the heavens become no longer only the house of the gods but also the means whereby one might carry on living on the surface of the earth. That does not mean that worship is not directed to the heavens. This is clear from temples where there is evidence of both worship and of technical observations. In fact, from the terraces of the temples the priests carried out the astronomical observations to determine the rising and setting of the sun and its path across the sky, the appearance and disappearance of the stars, and the rhythmic dance of the planets on the deep blue sky. Still, despite the emergence of this technical sense of the heavens, there remained a unity to the cosmos because everything spoke of the divine. The fundamental approach was that of the mythical, whereby one learns to read the invisible and numinous in the visible.

The regularity and predictability of heavenly motions gave rise, on the other hand, to the tendency to measure and to predict. This was a first indication of a scientific approach to nature. This new point of view is seen in the first calendars, which, in some instances, were very like our own. Not less indicative of this approach is the architecture of both civic and religious buildings. A knowledge of the positions of the sun, the moon, and the stars was required to determine the foundations of buildings, whether apartment building, tomb, or temple. In this way there arose the need to have descriptions of natural data which were directly applicable to everyday needs. To do this required going from a description tied to myth to a measurement which was intended to provide a quantity which described what was observed in an objective way. We have here the beginning of the desire to know how things function, even though such an intention was not explicit as we know it today.

This way of looking at the sky becomes ever more necessary, even for our ancestors, since in order to live they were learning how to interact with nature in its various forms. The result of all of this is to create a new mentality, a new way of viewing things which will slowly but surely lead to a change in ways of both doing and thinking. Looking at the sky has more to do with how matters will develop than one might at first think.

The Cosmology of the Egyptians

In Egypt it is mostly practical motives which give birth to science and mathematics. It was necessary to establish times for divine worship and for prayers for the dead, to know when the floods came and, therefore, when to sow and to reap. Thus will come the calendar and the division of the day into twelve hours. Let us see how this happened. The Egyptians' principal god was Amon-Ra, the sun god. Since this god was central to their worship they naturally wanted to study his motion on the horizon, his rising and setting and the solstices. He was the son of the goddess Nut, who was represented as a woman encircling the vault of the heavens. Amon-Ra entered her mouth at the spring equinox and was born nine months later at the winter solstice. At sunset as Amon-Ra went down below the horizon he entered into Duat, the zone of the dead, and spent the night there on the solar boat. The trip was marked by twelve gates (the twelve hours of the night), at each one of which he had to recite correctly certain preset formulas which allowed him to pass through. But when was he to recite these formulas? The answer, of course, was when certain stars or groups of stars appeared on the horizon. Thus was born a sidereal clock whose time intervals were set by the rising of twenty-four different stars.

Amon-Ra's journey through the heavens was repeated cyclically, and 365 days were required for him to return to his birthplace on the southeastern horizon at the winter solstice. This determination was made in the year 4500 B.C.E. It was also necessary to fix the dates of religious feasts, particularly those involved in Amon-Ra's birth. For that reason in the delta or Lower Egypt a lunar calendar was composed made up of twelve months of twenty-nine or thirty days each. However, this did not square with the cycle of Amon-Ra, and so every two or three years eleven intercalary days were inserted.

There were various problems in Upper Egypt where agriculture was linked to the flow of the Nile, which seemed to be regulated by heliacal (near the sun) rising of the star Sirius. In 4500 B.C.E. Sirius rose heliacally when the Nile began to increase near the beginning of June. But this calendar also had irregularities. Consequently, a calendar was set up with twelve months each of thirty days and it was divided into three seasons each of four months, corresponding to the periods of sowing, reaping, and flooding. Five days were added at the beginning, thus completing the cycle and making it equivalent to that of Amon-Ra.

Timekeeping also influenced the construction of temples. Their specific orientation toward certain groups of stars can be explained only by the fact that it was necessary to measure with a certain degree of precision the time of rising during the night of various groups of stars. In this way they determined intervals of sixty minutes each. Other details of timekeeping could be discussed, but what we have seen already makes the point. We have not yet arrived at truly scientific endeavors since everything, even the routines of daily existence, is seen in terms of relationships with the gods, who oversee all aspects of the life of each person and of the community.

The Viewpoint of the Assyrians and Babylonians

For the first time we find among these peoples, especially the Babylonians, systematic observations of the moon and the planets. This claim is supported by archeological finds and by ephemerides of the new moon which have even been discovered. These meticulous observations were, however, not made for scientific purposes but rather in support of astrology, a pursuit of prime importance in the world of Mesopotamia. Astrology can be seen as one of the ways whereby our ancestors sought to relate to the gods. On the one hand, it expressed in some way the experience that human beings were fundamentally inadequate in the face of the phenomena of nature. On the other hand, it proposed that the gods sent forth warning signals about the future and that humans could make use of these signals if they knew how to observe and interpret them. This way of thinking will have a lasting influence, even to our own day, on the journey of the human spirit. Considering all of the technical and scientific knowledge available to us today, it is of significance to note that people still have recourse to astrology in order to know the future. This may be an indication that scientists do not dialogue well with the common people of our times and do not respond to their queries in a manner proper to the sciences. Here is a Babylonian text which is fundamental to astrology:

> Earthly events are signs for us. Both heaven and earth produce portents. Even if they appear to be separate, in reality they are not, because heaven and earth are intertwined.

The interpretation of these signs was, therefore, vital for the well-being of the people. But the process of interpreting was reserved to the king, since he was the only one responsible for the good of the nation. As an official duty he fixed each year the subdivisions of the calendar and the number of months contained in each. He was supplied with data by a group of astronomers and astrologers whose duty it was to make systematic observations of the heavens. Of particular interest were the moon at the beginning and end of the month and the heliacal rising and setting of the planets and their position among the constellations. Based on these observations the king decided not only about the calendar but also about political and military events.

Despite the precision of the observations and the mathematical analysis used to predict celestial phenomena, the purpose was not scientific but rather to establish and maintain good relationships between the nation and the gods. Much time will pass before this linkage between observations of the heavens and religion will be broken. The movement in that direction will occur with the Greeks, relying upon the traditions of the Egyptians, and especially the Babylonians.

The Approach of the Hebrew Peoples

It is in the Bible, especially in the first chapters of Genesis, that we find how the Hebrew peoples viewed the cosmos. There are many particulars in the creation accounts of Genesis which show that, far from being completely original, the Jewish people rely upon cosmogonic myths of neighboring cultures, especially those of the Egyptians. Nevertheless, the Genesis accounts have distinguishing features. The creative act in the other traditions was seen exclusively as an act of bringing order out of preexisting chaos. In Genesis there is a richer presentation. While the act of ordering is still there, the notion of creating from nothing is dominant and is not found at all in neighboring cultures. Another peculiarity of the creation accounts in the Bible is that they come about not through some action such as those of an artisan, who models something out of the formless or reassembles something that is in disarray, but rather through the pronouncement of words. The God of the Bible creates by speaking, or, better said, God's words are such that they put into being that which they express. This act of creating by the word implies an interlocutor. This means that in the Hebrew culture, and later on in Christianity, the creative act, be it to begin something from nothing or be it a reordering, is always a dialogue. It looks to establishing a relationship with a "you," with the "other." This appears to be a key factor in a correct interpretation of the creation accounts. There is another important difference. While for other cultures the gods often took on the form of stars or other heavenly bodies, for the Hebrews the heavenly bodies have only the role of illuminating day and night and so there is nothing divine about them.

Apart from these remarks little can be said about cosmology in the Bible. It is principally a theological reflection on the world's beginning and on the value of creation in relationship to humankind. It is not a particularized description of how things happened. This becomes even clearer when we realize that the whole Bible is a theological reflection upon the relationship of the Hebrew people to their God, a relationship which included everything and, therefore, included the role and the value of nature both in itself and as it related to human beings. Nor must we forget that these reflections occurred after the Hebrews had settled down in the promised land and had, therefore, come to know their God as a savior and liberator. Starting from this way of seeing their God and how he related to them, they organized the creation accounts which, therefore, are accounts of salvation history rather than detailed and historically dependable descriptions of what actually occurred at creation.

Even if they are not very relevant to science, these accounts are valuable. They are, in fact, a good example of exactly what we are attempting to do, namely, to reflect upon the meaning of things, including scientific results, in order to discover whether, indeed, nature can speak to us, not only through the physical and mathematical descriptions of it, but also through the emotional and sense experiences which it arouses in those who observe and study it. The creation accounts are also a first attempt at synthesizing what we know, so that in the end it becomes not only knowledge but wisdom, and thus makes living a much richer experience.

This approach to the biblical accounts seems, while respecting science and scientific results, to respond to the message which the Bible wishes to convey. It wishes, we repeat, to offer an interpretation of the meaning of things and not just a mechanical explanation of how they work, although respecting the latter.

An Opening to the World of the Greeks

As we move on to the world of the Greeks we come for the first time to a cosmology, as compared to what has been thus far a cosmogony. The emphasis is no longer on the divine origins of the cosmos but rather on describing the cosmos from what we observe of it. Cosmogony was really theology, a reflection about how the world came to be from the gods. Cosmology will be different.

A different language will be required, a language more appropriate to this new venture. And so we will have the first professional astronomers and the first philosophers. As the name implies, the astronomers will seek to know the laws governing the cosmos. The philosophers will attempt to reflect upon the foundations of the universe itself. We must direct our attention to these two approaches to the cosmos and compare the outcome of these two ways of thinking. Together with astronomy we witness the rise of philosophy, and it will play a significant part for a number of centuries until the scientific method marches onto the stage. We might even say that philosophy will, to a great extent, take over for a period of time the role played thus far by theology.

~ *Chapter Two* ~

THE PATHWAY
OF THE GREEKS

T HEOLOGICAL REFLECTIONS on the cosmos are little by
little giving way to philosophical discourse. It is interesting to try to understand how that happened and
why this occurred in Greece.

This change has its roots far back and begins with the
Mesopotamian and Egyptian civilizations, where one begins to see that the need to measure time is no longer
linked to worship but rather to the cultivation of the
earth. It becomes increasingly clear, in fact, that one
needs a calendar which is useful and is not varying all
the time and which, moreover, is the same for the entire
country and not different for different regions. We have
already seen how in Mesopotamia and Egypt such a calendar, in fact, existed, even though in those civilizations
the calendar remained tied to the gods.

With the Greeks the desire for uniformity became ever
more pressing, and so astronomy began to take on a
purely practical character. It was no longer a question
of knowing or foreseeing the changeable humors of the
gods but rather of knowing when the time was propitious
for sowing, for pruning, for the harvest, and when cer-

tain festivities should be celebrated. Here is a text from Hesiod's *Works and Days:*

> When the Pleiades, daughters of Atlas, rise,
> begin to sow,
> and when they set,
> begin to plow.

There is no longer any religious reference to the observations of the heavens. It is all a mere question of agriculture. In the wake of this purely agricultural approach such figures as Meton, Hipparchus, and Ptolemy prepared catalogs of the principal astronomical phenomena and attempts were made by them to predict the weather. Although we cannot yet speak of astronomy as a science, the data in these catalogs were due to an analysis of direct observations of the heavens. This was a sign that such observations were no longer under the power of the priestly caste but belonged to professional astronomers. A kind of "lay" thinking was coming to be, a different way of viewing the heavens, which would be expressed most eloquently by the Pre-Socratics. In the observations and descriptions of the heavens they began to ask questions such as those which any scientists today would make: What are the heavenly bodies made of? What causes their motions? How are they related to the earth? Why do they behave the way they do?

We can gather that the heavens were no longer the dwelling place of the gods or a manifestation of their activities when we read the following definition of the heavens by Anaximander of Miletus, who wrote in the first half of the sixth century B.C.E.:

> The stars [for him this meant all heavenly bodies includ-
> ing the planets, the sun, and the moon] come to be as
> spheres of fire, separated out from the fire of the universe
> and confined by air. There are some holes in the celestial
> sphere which allow us to see the stars and when these
> holes are covered eclipses occur.

This new way of viewing the heavens opened the way to
a new interpretation of what happened there. Thus Par-
menides can assert that the moon is illuminated by the
sun and that the earth is spherical. Empedocles claims
that eclipses of the sun are caused by the passage of the
moon in front of it. Democritus has the suspicion that
there are other planets. This growing movement toward
the search for a universe which was less supernatural
and more rational finds in the Ionian seafarers of the
sixth century B.C.E. the beginnings of a new school of
thought about the heavens. Thus the universe for them
could function not only according to the will of the gods
but also according to the laws of mechanics and physics which could be understood by study and which could
be used to make predictions. The text of Anaximander
quoted above is just one obvious example of an attempt
to explain the universe in terms of physics, even though
it was just a vague theory of how things worked. The
knowledge which came to the Ionians from Mesopotamia
contributed much to advance this way of thinking. As
we have seen, the attempts of the Mesopotamians to describe celestial events and their repetitivity had been very
fruitful.

In parallel with this new way of viewing the heavens
we have, especially in Athens, the development of geom-

etry, which became of prime importance for describing celestial phenomena and even more important for developing geometrical models of those phenomena. This is an important moment because nature, and in particular the heavens, is becoming an object for laboratory experiments. The elaboration of models means that we are becoming ever more confident that we can deepen our knowledge of that which up until now had been considered to be an unfathomable secret. Moreover, this is beginning to lead us little by little to distinguish among science, philosophy, and theology as different ways of reflecting upon the cosmos. The cosmos could still be the home of the gods, but as to investigating it with physics, the cosmos was independent of them. Thus physics is coming to be, at this time only germinally, a discipline in its own right with respect to other sectors of human knowledge.

Nature herself seems to be taking on a new face in that she allows herself to be modeled descriptively by geometry. We can already see another problem on the horizon for both physics and philosophy, and it will become more important as time goes on. What is the nature of geometry? What do we mean by the laws of physics and of mathematics? Today this is becoming an ever more acute problem as cosmological theories, one after the other, propose models to explain the very first phases in the evolution of the visible universe. Put simply the problem is the following: Is nature itself mathematical, written with mathematics, or is it that we find it convenient to deal with nature by using mathematics? The question is obviously a key one. If the answer leans to-

ward the first alternative, mathematics becomes a kind
of metaphysics.

At any rate, thanks to this new view of the cosmos an
opportunity is offered for the first time in fourth-century
B.C.E. Greece to formulate a cosmology. The earth is at
the center of a universe which is spherical. It in turn is
spherical and without motion. At the ultimate bound-
ary of the universe there is the sphere of the fixed stars
which rotates around the earth from east to west carrying with it all of the heavenly objects which are located
between the earth and this sphere. These bodies which
lie in between — the sun, the moon, and the planets —
rotate in turn spherically but in the opposite direction.

This first attempt at cosmology soon had to face facts
which it could not explain. The planets, in fact, had a
retrograde motion, while both the moon and the planets
wandered north and south with respect to the passage
of the sun. Eudoxus first proposed a tentative solution
by making use of geometry. The results were satisfactory
for those times but were fraught with intrinsic errors.
Such attempts emphasized the point that underlying the
observed data another question was lurking. How did the
models relate to the observations? And especially, how
did established models relate to new ones?

It is interesting to note, even to emphasize, that we are
seeing here the beginning of a way of thinking whereby
the geometrical model becomes and remains critical. It
must be preserved and kept up to date. The model must
be continuously corrected and adjusted according to the
observations. In this series of corrections we see a tension
arising between the old and the new. This tension will

become a driving force to progress in the sciences and will make the natural sciences the least dogmatic, perhaps, of human intellectual endeavors. Science will survive and will mature whenever it accepts the need to go down into the arena and face new discoveries which question and criticize what it has already accomplished. An early example of this can be seen in Aristotle's acceptance of the model of Eudoxus corrected by Callipus.

The poet Arato in his work *Phenomena* immortalized the ideas of Eudoxus, and so they became the principal source for the Greeks to come to know the heavens. Nevertheless, we note another interesting point from a careful reading of the works of Arato. While it is true that the separation between a religious and a scientific way of viewing the cosmos is becoming solidified, the two ways of thinking will still have to coexist for centuries. It will take time before we can hear from the mouth of Galileo, who quotes Cardinal Caesar Baronius, that it is one thing to know how the heavens go and another to know how to go to heaven. The beginning of Arato's poem makes this quite clear:

> We start from the heavens! We humans never cease to invoke the heavens. Every place and byway where people gather are full of heaven, as are the sea and its havens. In every need we have recourse to heaven. After all, we are its creatures. And benign heaven indicates to each one his opportunities and awakens all peoples to their tasks reminding them of the means whereby they sustain their lives. It tells us when the turf is ready to be turned by the oxen and with the plow; it tells us what seasons are most propitious for pruning the trees and for sowing seeds of all kinds. It imprinted the signs in the heavenly vault, dividing up the stars and wisely distributing the constel-

lations throughout the year so as to signal to mankind the best times of the seasons so that everything could grow strong and healthy. And so men invoke the heavens at the beginning and at the end.

The significance of this whole affair started by the Greeks was to abandon once and for all the mythical and metaphorical view of the world and to take up a view which was tied to the concepts of necessity and of cause and effect. The use of geometry and the introduction of modeling, however primitive, indicates the start of this process which will bring about not only a new global conception of the cosmos but also a new way of understanding life and our relationship to the divine.

Greek Thought and the Judaeo-Christian Culture

What the Greeks had accomplished had already been attained in a different way by the Jewish peoples. The attempt there to detach the heavens from the divine is clearer, though less definitive. But the way in which the Greeks accomplish this is different. For the Greeks geometry is the driving force; for the Hebrews it is their faith in one God. We should not ignore at this point the first attempts by the newborn Christian religion to bring about a synthesis between these two different approaches. In fact, for the Jewish people reflection on the cosmos did not have its origins in observations, but rather in their history. They had been freed from slavery by their God and so they sought to worship him by praising him in the cosmos and all that was in it. It was from this reli-

gious perspective that the Jewish people began to think
about creation and the significance of the cosmos. They
did this with a language which would allow their read-
ers to realize that the universe was more the result of
God's love toward humankind than it was of physical
laws. In contrast, the Greek way of thinking was, as we
have seen, that there was, indeed, a rationality in the
universe to be discovered by observing physical phenomena. We might say that, while Hebrew culture sought the
why of things, the Greeks were for the most part inter-
ested in what made things work. Christianity was born
in the cultural context of Judaism. But it was very much
influenced by Greek culture and, in fact, very early in
its history its sphere of action and influence moved from
Palestine toward the West, first to Greece and then to
Rome. Through their meeting with the masters of Greek
thought the first Christian preachers were forced to the
task of adapting their message to the Greek way of thinking. All of Western culture, and so the development of
science, has been definitively influenced by this meeting.
In fact, in many ways, science is the daughter of this synthesis. Our knowledge of reality, and most importantly
our knowledge of ourselves, will be the beneficiaries of
this synthesis.

In the Greek world there is a maturing of the idea
that nature has laws which are fixed and not subject to
the whims of the gods. Between cause and effect there
is insinuated the idea of necessity. Among the Hebrews
this view of things is not so explicit, although there are
indications that it is present in a subdued manner. We
can garner some idea of it from their notion of mira-

cle or prodigy. One can think of a "mirum," something about which to wonder, as an exception to the laws of nature only if nature has laws. We no longer have miracles as exceptions if everything is seen as a manifestation of the will of the gods. In that case everything is a miracle. But if everything is a miracle, then in the end there are none. For the Hebrews miracles implied laws of nature, although they did not explicitly assert this.

The Great Greek Philosophers

Let us elaborate on the idea of necessity. If nature is subject to certain laws, then every happening is the consequence of a kind of necessary process which causes the phenomenon to happen every time there exist the conditions required for it to happen. That an event occurs every time the correct conditions are present must mean that in nature there are connections which can be described mathematically and expressed in mathematical language. This was the exceptional discovery which opened the way to the abandonment of the mythical view of the world, even though, as we have seen, the separation between the two views was not altogether clear. In fact, the two approaches, far from excluding one another, could best be understood in tension with one another.

The philosophical reflections of Plato, and especially those of Aristotle, have their origins here. They could not ignore the ideas developed previously by the Pythagoreans nor the teaching about being of the Greeks. If being is an unchangeable reality, thought Plato, the reality of all events in nature consists only of appearances. Here we have only representations of ideas and forms that belong to a separate, immaterial world which, for the most part, remains inaccessible to our knowledge. Plato placed the objects of mathematics among these perfect forms and thus set up the possibility and the necessity of a mathematical description of natural phenomena.

Being much more pragmatic Aristotle would not accept the existence of a world of ideas. He concentrated on the notions of cause and effect as derived from the world of sense experience. His was an inductive method which allowed one to uncover the "form" of the objects in nature. A mathematical form was among these, and it became known by studying the physical properties of objects, i.e., their number, dimension, and shape.

On the other hand, Archimedes initiated an approach that was both mathematical and empirical by applying mathematics not *a priori* as Plato did but *a posteriori* as a means of discovering the existing relationships in nature by observations and experiments. As we have already anticipated, this process made no small contribution to a new view of the world of the gods, even to the point that Anaximenes claimed that it was not the gods who helped us to investigate and understand nature, but it was nature that explained the gods. The next step was taken by Heraclitus, who located in a "logos" the principle of unity in nature. This "logos" was a kind of foundation of the rational order in the world and was not to be sought in religious worship.

The gods, therefore, assumed another appearance. They were no longer able to explain nature; they were, in fact, products of nature and in particular of human beings; and so they had the same character as humans and, like them, were mortal. We might note here how monotheism comes to light as the only form of religion compatible with the new way of viewing nature. Xenophon makes this point when he says that, if there is a God, he must be

> ...one, the greatest among the gods and among men, completely different than mortals both in form and in thought.

Still, it was necessary to make more explicit and to deepen these new principles which had the capacity to give a new unity to our description of nature.

Plato had attempted this by proposing that creation came about by a demiurge who gave *logos* to that which was *alogos* and measure to that which was *ametros*. In this way order was drawn from the original chaos. Subsequent to this first creative act there followed the creation of the lower gods, among them Zeus. But the demiurge was not to be identified with the supreme being, even less so with a god whose actions were determined by eternal, preexisting ideas, of which nature is only an imperfect image.

Aristotle approached the problem by having recourse to the idea of causes, and he came to the hypothesis of a first cause on which all others depended. This he called the first mover, which had to be unchangeable, immaterial, perfect, and intelligent, and which existed by necessity, i.e., it could not not exist. But was this a personal God or rather a God of the philosophers? Aristotle himself must have been perplexed by such questions, since he supported the erection of images of Zeus and Athena.

But still there remained a doubt as to whether the idea of causes could provide the ultimate explanation. For Socrates the answer was obvious. In the end the scientific enterprise is irrelevant to fulfill the highest aspirations of humankind. In fact to achieve those aspirations one must abandon science so as not to get lost in the labyrinth of phenomena. This is not a new idea, since we know that in the east with Buddhism similar steps had already been taken and, driven to their ultimate extreme, they could lead to a position that nature was radically unknowable and that we are slaves of the appearances of things, the phenomena. Paradoxically the fear of losing oneself in phenomena brought about an enslavement to them. It is difficult, especially for the Western mentality, to share such a position. Among the highest aspirations in the West is knowledge as an expression of that which is most human. This knowledge might also lead to control and management of some of nature's forces from which we must defend ourselves. Even though science might not be able to give us ultimate answers, its contribution to identifying final causes could be an important help in the pursuit of wisdom.

The problem now became quite a bit clearer. The mythological view of the world is gone. There is a new approach, philosophical and germinally scientific. What place in all of this is there for religion? There were indications of "cooperation." There was no denying that the new approach to nature could have significance for religion, even though it was not clear what that might be.

A Deepening of the Concept of Cosmos

What we have briefly reviewed brings us to reconsider and deepen the notion of cosmos, to ask about its destiny, should there be such, and about the search for perfection. The answers to these questions have not solely and exclusively a scientific importance. They move us, rather, to read in subtle print the religious implications underlying the scientific description of nature.

The idea of "cosmos," so dear to the Greeks, contains certain elements that might be of help to us in our voyage. It provides a happy wedding between the notions of order and of harmony. The order of the cosmos arose from the Greek philosophers with their idea of cause and effect, employing a geometrical model of the world and the creation of the world as an image of the world of ideas, imperfect as that creation might be. Harmony was also the fruit of mathematical models. The precursor of this idea was Pythagoras, who saw in the motions of heavenly bodies a musical symphony which could be re-created in simple numerical relationships.

But a deeper study of the heavens showed that there were irregularities and imperfections. It would be difficult to explain these with a symphonic view of the universe. How, moreover, was one to reconcile the conceived perfect heavens with the obvious imperfections on the earth? All subsequent efforts were dedicated to saving the perfect heavens. Models of the universe, culminating in that of Ptolemy, bear witness to the fact that for the Greeks, and later for Hellenism, the idea of cosmos could not be renounced. It was, in fact, precisely the idea of "cosmos" which provided the key to identify the unifying principle of the universe.

As we have already seen, there was added to this idea, even if by different paths, that of the Hebrew people, who embraced monotheism, a living reality and not just an idea. Furthermore, unlike that of the Greeks, whose monotheism was just beginning, theirs was a personal God. For the Jews the God who created the world was a person, and it was this personal God who called them to a personal relationship. And if the Greek philosophers claimed that it was not in worship that one came face to face with the unifying principle of the world, the Jewish claimed just the opposite. To meet personally the God who had revealed himself in their history was to meet not only the Creator but also the one who sustained nature in a mutual relationship with it. Creation for the Jewish people happened by the word. Word implied dialogue. Dialogue by its very nature implied two parties who are not gods, but creator and created. No longer are creatures powerless spectators. Humankind becomes a cocreator and one of the reasons for creation.

Ptolemy's cosmology, which puts the earth at the center of the known universe, expresses the fact that the human, dweller on the earth, has a unique role in the cosmos. This idea will pass to the Christian world and will become explicit in Western theology. Still we must not forget that, even if this represents an attempt to carry forward the unification which Greek philosophy had intuited, that attempt at unification will also be the harbinger of mistaken notions which will haunt us down through the centuries.

Nor was the Latin world a stranger to the spirit which gave life to ancient Greek culture. At least it owed to the Greeks the intellectual formation of the most important personages in its culture. On the other hand we must recognize that the character and the interests of the Latin world were not as all-embracing and did not seek to go in depth into every branch of knowledge as did the Greek intellectuals. The attention of the Latins was drawn more to law and to history with such great personages as Cicero, Tacitus, and Caesar. There were also schools of philosophy where many Roman emperors studied. Eminent among them was that of Seneca. Science was touched upon but more for the sake of poetry than of science itself. Thus Lucretius became famous for his poem *De rerum natura,* although all he did was to repeat the reflections and the knowledge that came from Greece. He may have added a bit of philosophy but certainly no science.

~ Chapter Three ~

TOWARD A CREATOR
OF THE CREATED

T HERE IS LITTLE DOUBT that the worldview generated by Ptolemy dominated all thinking up until the time of Copernicus. That does not mean that observations of the heavens ceased, but only that the fundamentals of astronomy were fixed and no longer questioned. At most they could be perfected. Nonetheless, this was the time in which the seeds were being sown for Copernicus and later for Galileo to come forth with new theories and a new worldview. It was not, as is sometimes thought, a period of stagnation, but new views were slowly coming to life in the embers which consumed old worldviews and enkindled new ones.

In discussing this period of history we will be forced to deal in more detail with the development of the philosophy of nature and with those sciences which in the past had been indispensable to the growth of astronomy: mathematics, physics, and geometry.

Culture and Its Institutions

Among the most important institutions of that time, and so one that merits our attention, is that of monasticism.

39

There were very few persons who were truly cultured, and those few found immense difficulty in dealing with the ancient texts, most of which were written in Greek. And so the works of the great masters in philosophy, such as Plato and Aristotle, or those in astronomy, such as Ptolemy, ran the risk of remaining as works written but not read. At this critical point enter the monks. Their work of recopying the ancient manuscripts is recognized to be of enormous importance in preserving the roots of Western culture since those manuscripts are known to be the very roots of the renaissance of that culture. They realized that, apart from being a privileged few, they had a duty to society, since they were the few fortunate ones able to read and write in a world that for the most part was illiterate. They had the task of preserving that incomparable treasure of knowledge stored up in the works, at times original, at times in translation, of the wise men of old. They were, as Christianity has always been, at the service of culture. At that time, it was an extremely precious and delicate task that they performed.

We must not forget that the first universities came to be only in the thirteenth century and that before then, at least in the West, education in philosophy, theology, and the natural sciences was substantially in the hands of Church institutions. We should not, therefore, be surprised that the scientists of that period were all Churchmen. The lack of real science, often attributed to that time, is illusory. In fact, a new way of viewing nature was slowly being born. A new institution, the university, was coming to be. It expressed a kind of frenzy to make more universally accessible the knowledge that until then had been in the hands of the Church and that seemed to cry out for more room than was allowed to it. It needed to break loose and bring to fruition the hidden riches it possessed.

The spread of Christianity brought with it a fundamental belief in a unique Creator of heaven and earth and, therefore, a firm denial of many gods and spirits, who had until then been thought to be the source of all phenomena. This opened the way to a scientific approach to nature. One of the pioneers in this scientific approach was Isidore of Seville with his twenty volumes of *Etymology,* a text which, although not altogether correct scientifically, nonetheless showed that nature could be described in a language free of myth and mythology. As a first result distinctions were drawn between astronomy and astrology, the former being seen as a true science while the latter gradually became ostracized as pure superstition. This was an important step, if for no other reason than that it gave back to the human being that freedom of thought which had, perhaps even unconsciously, been surrendered to the fates.

This freedom of the intellect, newly rewon, flourished at the monastery and cathedral schools throughout Europe, where the seven liberal arts, divided into the *trivium* (grammar, rhetoric, and logic) and *quadrivium* (arithmetic, geometry, music, and astronomy), were taught. It is significant that astronomy was part of the curriculum and that, in teaching it, use was made of manuals and textbooks which attempted to bring about a unification of what was known.

At the same time in Islam there was a flourishing

culture dedicated to the translation of the works of the ancient Greeks into the Arab languages. These translations arrived in Europe by means of the Arab conquest of Spain. In this way Western culture could see on the horizon a new period of growth. In fact, a large part of this cultural patrimony was already by the year 1200 translated into Latin. Cultural pursuits in Europe were beginning to mature. Evidence of this is provided by the rise of the various schools which specialized in the diverse areas of human knowledge: law at Bologna, medicine at Montpellier, theology at Paris, natural philosophy at Chartres. Very soon, however, these specialized studies at a given place began to grow into a multiplicity of studies at a given place. Thus was born the university. Studies in the various disciplines were structured in such a way that, in order to arrive at the higher levels of learning, one had to go through the *trivium* and *quadrivium*. Thus, elementary studies in the seven liberal arts were required of anyone who wished to arrive at the higher levels of university education.

This system of education might appear to be trivial. However, it reveals in reality a search for a unified knowledge of reality and thus a view that nature itself possessed a wholeness. Priority, of course, had been given to philosophy and theology with the result that scientific approaches were rudimentary and rather imprecise. But the unity of human knowledge, reflecting the unity of the universe itself, was in good hands. This unity was even further advanced by the relationship of philosophy as being at the service of theology, a relationship which was well recognized by each of those disciplines. These priorities among the disciplines should not surprise us. There was a radical conviction at that time that beyond the appearances there lay a single animating force and that, since this force was god-like, it was most comprehensively understood by those disciplines which, by their very nature, dealt with such entities. In light of this way of thinking mathematics became the language to describe the universe, an inheritance from Archimedes, for whom the task of science was to discover the mathematical relationships among the factual data of experienced and observed phenomena.

Thomas Aquinas and Aristotle

But sooner or later Aristotle's influence would have to make itself felt. He, as we know, had a different approach to understanding nature. For him it meant coming to a knowledge of the causes of phenomena, and this conception lay at the basis of his philosophical treatise *De coelo*. It was, perhaps, precisely the use in the universities of this treatise on the heavens which opened the way to discovering both physical and metaphysical answers to questions about the structure of the universe. Undoubtedly this approach had many advantages, one of which was to provide a unifying knowledge to multifaceted questions; but hidden within it were also some problems which would only gradually come to light, and sometimes with damaging repercussions.

Furthermore, its non-Christian origins weighed heavily on Aristotle's conception of the world, and this made it all the more difficult to reconcile his thought with a culture which by this time had been for centuries dominated by Christian theology. It was to be an Italian Dominican monk who would bring about the synthesis which would draw Aristotle back into prominence. Thomas Aquinas brought back, in fact, the ideas of Aristotle on the natural world and thus provided a cosmology which for centuries would direct Western thinking on the universe, a conception which did not, it must be said, give a great deal of importance to scientific data. At most, being open only to that which up until then was considered true, it limited the truth value of the data themselves to that which one might seek from biblical-theological studies and rather excluded data from the sciences. Matters were to become, as the reader may already intuit, a bit complicated. It would soon become clear that a breath of fresh air would have to penetrate this castle of learning, which, for all of its apparent solidity, would, with the onslaught of the beginnings of modern science, begin to show its many weaknesses and would come to be seen as much more fragile than was even conceivable at that time. But all of us thrive on certainty, and the Aristotelian-Thomistic approach was, indeed, capable of providing such intellectual security. But, one who honestly seeks the truth is also recognized by his conviction that the truth is always a goal to be reached, that it is always a bit beyond our grasp. As one travels that path toward the truth, a path which may open into many side roads, one becomes aware that it is necessary to question what has appeared up until then to be solidly and indisputably true. Such is the path to knowledge and to wisdom!

In those days the university made no claim to being an ambient for research; it was dedicated only to teaching. Research was carried on elsewhere, especially through the systematic translation of texts and the practice of logic. We should not forget that there was at that time a strong interest in the tools of astronomy and especially in the positional measurement of heavenly bodies. Indeed, if data were to be improved, so that our knowledge would become more abundant and truth-laden, it would be necessary to perfect the instrumentation needed to obtain better data. And so technology began its explicit collaboration with the sciences at the same time as it took paths which would allow it to develop in ways not directly linked to the aims of scientific research. It will, indeed, bring about significant achievements also in the world of esthetics and the arts. Once again we come to appreciate the outcome of a developing collaboration between various disciplines. These, for sure, are the first indications of a way of knowing which, even as it grows in specialization, still continues at its core to dialogue with other disciplines with the expectation that such dialogue will redound to the good of both science and technology.

Problems Remain

Difficulties arose, not so much from the measurements as from the reflections of philosophers who found themselves quite uncomfortable with the nonuniformity of heavenly motions which was required if one were to save Ptolemaic astronomy. Furthermore, there was the suspicion that the earth itself was not immobile but, as strongly indicated by the motion of projectiles, rotated on its own axis.

But these were not the only problems. Yes, it was true that Thomas Aquinas, by incorporating the spheres of Aristotle into the Christian view of the world, had provided a weighty synthesis of human knowledge and a very valuable and powerful tool for understanding the universe. But what about the spheres beyond the seven planets? And what about the motion of the sphere of the fixed stars? And, above all, how was this conception of the world related to, how could it be related to, the description found in the first book of Genesis on the creation of the world? And still more, what caused the motion of the heavenly spheres? God was the answer; God acted as the prime mover on the outermost of the spheres, but how could that be reconciled with the fact that God had given to each sphere a spiritual intelligence with the power to move every sphere by its own will? Times were, indeed, changing. Jean Buridan could introduce the idea of impetus, which had been held to be the cause of the motions of projectiles, as the cause also of the motion of the spheres. He thus avoided having the angelic intelligences involved by replacing them with an impetus which God himself is supposed to have given to each sphere at the moment of creation and which, in the absence of friction, would have been adequate to maintain the sphere in motion indefinitely.

Because of these doubts about Aristotelianism, philosophers were led to reexamine and to rethink the idea of necessity, since a Christian must now consider the will of the Creator who would have been free to make a different world. In others words Aristotelian necessity itself became contingent upon the will of the Creator. A new idea, due to Thomas Bradwardine, arose whereby to the infinity of God there must be a corresponding infinity of the universe. The finite firmament still defined the location of the world, but it was surrounded by an empty and infinite space which had a divine nature. A disciple of Buridan then proved that heavenly events would have appeared identical had one supposed that the earth rotated daily on its own axis.

These ideas were brought together into a further synthesis in 1440 by Nicolas of Cusa, for whom the universe was infinite, containing stars everywhere, and the earth was a "noble star" among all of the others. Every star rotated on its own axis so that any observer on whatever star would see an identical universe to the one observed from the earth. Only the axis of rotation and the poles would be different. This idea already resembles today's cosmological principle and as such is of some importance. It not only provides us a look back into the thinking of some in the Middle Ages, but it is also preparing the way for the substitution of the Ptolemaic-Aristotelian universe with a new view of the cosmos to be expressed by Copernicus in his *De Revolutionibus Orbium Coelestium*.

So That We Not Forget

After this brief summary of the historical record, we should evaluate some of the steps taken during our journey in the Middle Ages. The changes that were occurring have various roots. The spread of Christianity, as we have seen, made no small contribution to the formation of a new worldview. More and more the world was being seen as one governed by laws which could be expressed in the language of mathematics and physics, however rudimentary those expressions might be. Divine action, therefore, was no longer as omnipresent as it had been in the classic mythological descriptions of the universe. Then there was the movement to the West, transmitted by the Arabs, of all that had been inherited from classical Greek culture. This comprised not only new information, but also different ways of approaching natural phenomena. Our way of thinking today is undeniably due to those two currents, Greece and Christianity. This came about principally through the laborious dialogue between the two which brought forth in the end a synthesis. Greek culture had nurtured an appetite for enjoying the pleasure of thinking, reflecting, and investigating in a systematic way the phenomena of the universe. Christianity had provided a key to sensing the value of the role of human beings in this enterprise. It thus freed them from the slavery to which a lack of science, in the most comprehensive meaning of the term, had condemned them. They had been chained to the earth, forbidden to take flight toward the highest peaks, not only of science, philosophy, and religion, but also of true wisdom.

The birth of universities, which brought forth specialization in the various branches of learning, created a greater autonomy for each of the disciplines. However, at least as to astronomy and in particular the problem of the creation and existence of the world, undue importance was still given to the Bible as a source of ongoing investigation.

It was still, however, true that the Creator remained the principle of unity of the universe and that the search for its meaning belonged to theology. The other disciplines were at the service of theology. There apparently was at that time no dissatisfaction among researchers about this view, due perhaps to the impressive synthesis of Thomas Aquinas.

Another matter to be considered was the concerns of daily life where astronomy would serve to fix the calendar either for religious purposes (fixing the dates of religious feasts) or for material purposes (the seasons, the times for seeding and reaping, routes at sea). And even though philosophy, theology, and astronomy had banished astrology from the halls of true science, astrology still held sway in the mentality of the common people who, for a large variety of reasons, still had recourse to it.

The idea of the universe as a cosmos, inherited from ancient times, still lived on, not now with an order set by a pantheon of many gods but rather now by a unique and personal God. The harmony that reigned was taking on ever more the character of numbers, not any longer those of Pythagoras, but rather more closely allied to those of Archimedes where mathematics and physics were in alliance. The Creator himself was the one who provided assurance that the universe would remain orderly and harmonious even out to infinity.

The foundations had been laid. It would be the task of the scholars of the Renaissance to build upon this foundation and to meet the challenges which it provided.

~ *Chapter Four* ~

COPERNICUS
AND HIS REVOLUTION

I T IS DIFFICULT to appreciate all that is implied in the so-called revolution of Copernicus unless we look back over the preceding chapters and review in broad strokes the different ways of thinking about how science, our knowledge of the universe, was to be carried out.

The Pythagoreans, as early as six centuries before Christ in their centers of learning scattered along the Ionian coast, performed acoustical experiments in which they discovered that the intervals of the musical scale were related to the integer numbers. From these simple observations they developed mathematics as an important tool in the understanding of the universe, even to the extent that they attempted to discover a strict mathematical structure in the whole universe, a "harmony of the spheres," to explain the motions of all the then-observable celestial bodies by integer numbers and mathematical relationships among them. Mathematics was in its first stages of becoming the language of science.

Plato, Aristotle, Archimedes: Eternal Ideas and the World We Sense

Plato was profoundly influenced by the success of mathematics as a function of pure human reason to explain many natural phenomena, but he was also convinced that anything that was truly real had to be unchanging. The changeable and changing objects of this material world were not truly real but only images of a realm in which there were eternal unchanging ideas and forms, among which there were numbers, pure geometrical forms, and mathematical relationships. In Plato's view mathematics belonged to the realm of the eternal and the truly real; it preceded temporally, logically, and ontologically the imperfect images of the material world. Human reason was attuned to the mathematics of the truly real world and thus could detect the imperfect images of mathematics in the material world.

For Plato, therefore, science or knowledge of the material world necessarily involved mathematics, but mathematics existed eternally before the material world and independently of it. The use of the senses and experiments had nothing to do with true science and, in fact, could be quite deceptive in the attempt of human reason to discover the true mathematical forms and, therefore, the true nature of the universe.

In total contrast to this view, Aristotle, denying any separate world of ideas, claimed that all knowledge of the universe derives from experience, from what we sense. True, by abstraction from sense experience one derives the mathematical forms, which are, however, inherent in and not separate from material objects, and by further abstraction one comes to metaphysics and the knowledge of cause and effect. True science for Aristotle is the discovery of cause and effect, and his view has dominated science ever since. Science is the search for the causes of observed effects.

Must we choose between Plato and Aristotle? There is a third tradition which has its roots in the acoustical research of the Pythagoreans but which came to maturity with Archimedes and his experiments in mechanics. For Archimedes, unlike Plato, sense experience was primary and, like Aristotle, mathematics was essential to discovering relationships in nature. However, in contrast to Aristotle, science was not about discovering causes, a metaphysical concept, but simply about discovering the relationships in nature, expressed most meaningfully with mathematics. It was, in this way, a study of the nature of nature, the relationship of the parts to the whole.

The Real Significance of Copernicus

It is against this background of what science is, of how we know the universe, that we come to appreciate the real revolution of Copernicus's *De Revolutionibus Orbium Coelestium* and the contribution he thereby made to the birth of modern science, to the way we think about the universe today.

The true issues at hand, and for which Copernicus set the stage, had less to do with heliocentrism or geocentrism, with our geometrical or physical place in the universe, than with the relationship of ourselves as intelligent beings to the universe. How did we come to understand the universe? Copernicus prepared the way for the answer to that question, an answer which was to last down the centuries to our day. The answer would, however, as we shall soon see, leave the door open to exciting ventures in science, unforeseen and unforeseeable by himself or by his immediate followers.

Copernicus, of course, was not the first to propose that the sun was at the center of the universe and that all of the then-known "wandering objects," including the earth, went about it. Aristarchus, who flourished within the first half century after Plato, had already proposed such a picture. His principal reason for doing so was what he claimed to be the beauty of the system. While Copernicus embraces this idea of beauty, he also offers other arguments in support of his model.

The other arguments offered by Copernicus in favor of heliocentrism must be seen in contrast to the geocentric system of Ptolemy, which had dominated thinking about the universe since the publication of his voluminous *Almagest* in the second century after Christ. Both Copernicus and Ptolemy explained the observed phenomena by a complicated system of circular motions of the celestial objects, but the Copernican system was less complicated. Thus, in addition to beauty, simplicity was becoming a criterion for arriving at the best explanation of the phenomena.

We should pause here for a moment on the idea of simplicity. What is really meant is economy. One pays the least to get the most; one makes the fewest assumptions

to get the most explanatory power. It is always necessary to make assumptions, but the fewer they are and
the more intelligent they are, the more convincing is the
model proposed. Copernicus, for instance, assumed fewer
circular motions than Ptolemy, so his system was more
economical. Note, however, that Copernicus held to circular motions, an assumption inherited from the ancient
Greeks, for whom the circle was the perfect geometrical
figure and the only one befitting heavenly bodies which
were perfect. It will, as we shall see, take more than another half century before that assumption, prejudice we
could justly call it, is eradicated with Kepler's discovery
that elliptical orbits even further simplify the model. But
let us return to Copernicus.

In offering what he considered to be a beautiful and
simple (economical) system Copernicus, in a subtle way,
made a further claim which was to become a haunting re-
frain as subsequent protagonists, and principally Galileo,
moved toward the birth of modern science. Copernicus
claimed that his model was physically true; it was not
simply an explanation of the observed phenomena, but
it was what really happened in the universe. It was not
just a reasonable, mathematical way to view the universe;
it was actually what the universe did. In subtly intro-
ducing this claim Copernicus wove together the threads
of the three traditions on the nature of science about
which we have just spoken. Although not necessarily
with conscious determination, he emphatically denied
Plato's realm of the pure ideas and forms and insisted
that what was truly real was the universe as we experience it. He embraced Aristotle's assertion that sense

experience was primary and Archimedes' notion that mathematics was inherent in the universe we sensed. But he went further than any of them in claiming that the universe really and physically was as his mathematical formulations described it. The earth was not stationary in its "natural" place. It moved, and not with rectilinear but with circular motion, a motion, according to Aristotle, "natural" only to heavenly bodies. So, in his model, Copernicus, at least implicitly, denied a fundamental tenet of Aristotle, namely, that each element in the universe had a natural place and a natural motion and that there was a radical distinction between the earth and heavenly bodies. What Copernicus did here implicitly will become more explicit with those who follow him, especially with Galileo.

This break with Aristotelian natural philosophy, which had held almost undisputed sway for two millennia, was so daring and so abrupt that the final editor of Copernicus's epoch-making work, a Protestant preacher, Andreas Osiander, decided to publish a preface which, unbeknownst to Copernicus, denied precisely what Copernicus was proposing, namely, that his heliocentrism was a physical explanation of the way the real world was. Osiander told the reader that the system described in the book was a mere mathematical hypothesis and, as such, was no more probable than any other astronomical theory. An old thesis was being revived: astronomical theories had nothing to do with the real nature of the universe; they were merely mathematical constructs which helped to explain the observed phenomena. According to Osiander, Copernicus's system was no challenge to the natural philosophy (today we would say "physics") of Aristotle. But in reality, as we have seen above, it was. Copernicus, however, never witnessed the result of the revolution he had started. A copy of the *De Revolutionibus Orbium Coelestium* was for the first time placed in his hands as he was dying.

From Pure Mathematics to Physics

What Copernicus had started could not be snuffed out by any surreptitiously written preface. The march was on from geometry to physics. It would never again be enough to simply speak of mathematical models. Was the physical universe like Aristotle said it was: the realm of the heavens and the earthly realm, four fundamental elements each of which had a natural place and motion? or was it something else? There was not as yet even a glimmer of what that something else might be, but Copernicus had definitely set the challenge that it must be radically different from what Aristotle claimed.

Having accepted the challenge placed by Copernicus, how were we to come to know the physical nature of the universe? As it turns out, during the century after Copernicus through various unplanned historical circumstances and protagonists, chief among them being Tycho Brahe, Johannes Kepler, and Galileo Galilei, a combination developed of two of the great traditions about the very nature of science: the Aristotelian emphasis upon sense experience and the Archimedean insight into the mathematical nature of nature.

The great Danish astronomer Tycho Brahe, born three

years after the death of Copernicus, came to realize that the only way to resolve disputes about the true nature of the universe, Aristotelian or Copernican, was to obtain many more accurate observations of the motions of the planets. And so he constructed what was for his day the world's best equipped observatory, and he proceeded to assemble an immense catalog of data on the positions of the planets and the fixed stars. Later on Kepler, of whom we shall speak shortly, through a mathematical analysis of this data would establish the true nature of planetary orbits. Note the combination of accurate observations with mathematical analysis. The traditions of Aristotle and Archimedes are beginning to mature as they lead to the birth of modern science.

New Stars in the Heavens

While Brahe's voluminous observations were essential to the discoveries made by Kepler, his more fundamental contribution to our view of the universe came about rather by serendipity. A new star appeared in the sky just at the time that Tycho was at the prime of his ability to do accurate observations. From his observations he concluded that this new star was much more distant than any of the planets, the moon, or the sun and must belong to the realm of the fixed stars. Just as he reached this conclusion the new star disappeared from the sky. So, his observations could not be repeated or checked, but here was the first serious observational challenge to Aristotle's physics; the realm of the heavens was not immutable and unchangeable. It contained objects which appeared and disappeared. It is ironical that the method of sense experience which Aristotle championed came to be employed to destroy his own physical view of the universe. And then the heavens put on another show. Numerous comets appeared between 1577 and 1596, again precisely during the years when Brahe was best equipped to observe them. Again Brahe determined that they were very distant and, an even greater surprise, that they did not travel in circular orbits, but in elongated orbits, in fact, so elongated that they must pass through the various supposed celestial spheres of Aristotle.

Aristotle's fundamental "physics" of the universe, which called for separate realms of the heavens with celestial spheres, for the incorruptibility and immutability of the heavenly realm and for natural places and motions for the four basic elements, was beginning to collapse under the onslaught of the very technique which he had championed, the need for observations. This onslaught of observations will continue along its destructive path and culminate with the telescopic observations of Galileo, which we will soon discuss. Tycho Brahe had begun a process which would unceasingly lead to a revolution in our view of ourselves in the universe and to the birth of modern science.

The Size of the Universe: Brahe Confronts Copernicus

But Brahe could not bring himself, at this time in the history of scientific ideas, to accept Copernicanism. Why? To him Aristotelian physics was dead. Why not accept the view of Copernicus, modify it if observations so dictated, but break definitively from a sun-centered universe? It was precisely because of his fidelity to observations that Tycho could not embrace Copernicanism; he was not able to observe a parallax, a shift in the apparent position of the fixed stars, a necessary result of viewing the heavens from an earth which moved about the sun. The reason is, of course, that the distance of even the nearest stars is so much greater than the distance of the earth from the sun that the parallax is extremely small and was not measurable in Tycho's day. (Brahe could measure accurately to one arc minute, a great achievement for his day. The nearest star has a parallax of 0.8 arc seconds, about one hundredth of what Brahe could measure). But to accept this reasoning meant to accept that the universe was extremely large, that even the nearest of the fixed stars was more than one-quarter million times further away from the earth than the earth from the sun. This would also require, according to Tycho's observations of the sizes of stars, that many stars must be thousands of times larger than the sun. (His reasoning from his observations was wrong, since the phenomenon of diffraction was not yet known, but his conclusion that stars differ greatly in their sizes was correct.) He could not accept such an abrupt change in the nature of the universe, and so he proposed a hybrid system in which, indeed, the earth was at the center of the sphere of fixed stars, but all the planets went about the sun as it went about the earth.

It appears that in proposing this system Tycho was, at least implicitly, compromising and returning to the view that Osiander held with respect to Copernicus, namely, what was being proposed was a purely hypothetical mathematical model. It need not necessarily be the way the universe really was. Tycho's geometrical model simply reinforced the divorce inherited from antiquity between mathematics and natural philosophy, between a mere mathematical hypothesis and the real universe. At the same time his analysis of the comets and of the new star spoke to the physical nature of the universe and gave a death blow to the worldview of Aristotle.

Tycho Brahe is a splendid example of the tension that continued to exist in the birth pangs of modern science. No one would step forth and fully embrace both the Aristotelian and the Archimedean view of what science was all about: observations and experiment blended with mathematical analysis. We are on our way to a certain denouement in this tension. It will occur with Galileo. But, before we proceed, let us pause to reflect upon the significance of Tycho Brahe's hesitation to accept that the fixed stars could be at unimaginably large distances. Tycho's hesitation can teach us a great deal about our journey to understand ourselves in the universe.

Where Tycho Brahe hesitated, Giordano Bruno, a restless, intelligent Dominican friar who eventually left the monastery, boldly stepped forward and carried his allegiance to Copernicanism to an extreme. For him not only was the earth not at the center of the universe, but the universe itself was infinitely large and it contained an infinite number of worlds where there were many other planetary systems centered on suns like our own with planets like our earth; yes, even other intelligent beings. Unlike Brahe, Bruno never, as best we know, made a single detailed observation. Thus his ideas were pure speculation. He, therefore, contributed little or nothing to the movement toward the birth of modern science. But, even though he was outside the mainstream, it is of some interest to reflect upon the degree to which his ideas recur in our own day, but now with more observational evidence to support them.

It appears that our search for a knowledge of ourselves in the universe is never a straight path; we meander and wander, hopefully in the long run gaining more secure knowledge by confronting our ideas with careful observations and a mathematical analysis of them. At any rate, Giordano Bruno's end was not a pleasant one. He was burned at the stake, condemned by the Roman inquisition as a heretic for having taught, although he denied it, a kind of monism whereby the infinite universe and the infinite God were not easily distinguishable. Because Copernicanism was at the basis of his thinking, his condemnation cast a threatening shadow over any attempt to develop an understanding of the universe based upon the ideas of Copernicus.

But two factors contributed to the need for further observations and further mathematical analysis: first, the inadequacy of the several schemes, Ptolemaic, Tychonian, Copernican, which could to varying degrees be interpreted by some as being purely hypothetical, geometrical explanations of the observed phenomena; and second, the threats to the physics of Aristotle both by Copernicus's conviction that his was a true physical explanation and by Brahe's explanation of comets and of the new star. These needs were to be fulfilled, at least in part, by the researches of Kepler and of Galileo.

The New Astronomy of Kepler

Kepler (1571–1630) and Galileo (1564–1642) were contemporaries, and much of their productive scientific lives overlapped. They corresponded and exchanged many of their ideas, at times reluctantly on Galileo's part. Galileo, for instance, never accepted Kepler's discovery of elliptical orbits, one of the greatest breakthroughs in the entire history of astronomy and one that definitively did away with all of the geometrical shenanigans required by an exclusive allegiance to circular motions for heavenly objects. But they were very different personalities and had very different styles of carrying out research. In fact, their diverse styles provide an excellent example of how the so-called objectivity of the scientific method has, when it is actually practiced, many subjective, personal aspects to it.

Kepler was, in reality, somewhat of a mystic, and many of his writings are filled with religious symbolism which is very difficult to fathom. Although he did not embrace the Platonic world of ideas and forms as the truly real, he was strongly influenced by the metaphysics of the Pythagoreans, whereby preexistent mathematical forms became incarnate in the visible universe. He was fascinated by what he saw as the systematic, clock-like workings of the heavens, the celestial machinery, for which he was convinced there was a mathematical formulation.

As a young man he became an assistant to Tycho Brahe

and later succeeded him at Prague. He dedicated himself to mathematical analysis of the voluminous observations of Tycho and in 1690 published his epoch-making work, *The New Astronomy,* in which he formulated his first two laws of planetary motions: the planets move in elliptical orbits about the sun, which is located at one foci of the ellipse, and, as they do so, they move systematically faster the closer they are to the sun. This was truly a "new astronomy." While many challenges had been made, as we have seen, to the physics of Aristotle, here for the first time in the history of ideas a challenge was placed to the notion inherited from time immemorial that heavenly objects, being perfect, had to move in the most perfect of all geometrical figures, the circle. Furthermore, he made the extremely imaginative hypothesis that the laws of planetary motion which he had derived from Brahe's careful observations of Mars were universal and applied to all of the planets. He had no observational justification to make this claim for universality. It was an intuition, which, indeed, would be proven true.

How does Kepler's intuition about the universality of planetary motions differ, for instance, from that of Giordano Bruno about the infinity of universes? As we have seen and will continue to see, scientific knowledge progresses also by intuition, in addition to exact observations and careful mathematical analysis. How can we tell when an intuition is one that will lead to progress in knowledge? How can we tell whether to follow its lead or not? There is, as best we know, no clear and certain answer. But there are some indications. The best intuitions are those that have an observational basis. The intuition should be unifying, it should help bring to a resolution unanswered dilemmas that have been for a long time an obstacle to progress. And the intuition should lead even further beyond what it intuits. For instance, Kepler's intuition would lead eventually to Newton's law of universal gravitation. Kepler's intuition satisfied all of the above; Bruno's none of them. It is not, it would seem, an exaggeration to say that Kepler was the first of modern scientists. He used mathematical analysis of observations to uncover the relationships inherent in the universe, and he pushed beyond his immediate results to a more profound and provocative knowledge of the structures he had already discovered.

In Us the Universe Becomes Self-Reflective

Before we approach Galileo, let us, with what we know so far from history, confront the universe as intelligent beings within that same universe, curious about its nature. The very fact that we can do this is a marvel of the universe itself, a marvel so obvious that we cease to be amazed by it. In us the universe has become self-reflective; it can think about itself and try to understand itself. Whether we are alone as intelligent beings in the universe is a separate issue and an open one. The marvel is not that there might be intelligent life elsewhere in the universe; the real marvel is that there is intelligent life at all.

At the very beginning of human reflection on the universe, as we have seen in chapter 1, there was a dominant primitive view which saw the universe as full of personal forces, the gods and superpowers of nature.

We should, however, be careful not to attribute an exclusively negative character to the attribute "primitive." Such "primitive" notions are typically very pregnant with meaning and, when purified of what is patently false, frequently serve into the future to achieve an integrated and unified view of our place in the universe.

With the civilizations that flourished around the Ionian Sea for more than a half century there was a growing consensus that, rather than innumerable personal forces acting somewhat capriciously in the universe, the universe had an intrinsic rational structure, that all parts of it were interrelated to form a complex totality to whose rational structure human intelligence was attuned. But how precisely did this tuning come about?

Copernicus and those who followed in the century after him made a significant contribution to answering this very important question, a question which has a great deal to do with how we view ourselves as part of this complex universe. Relying on the intellectual traditions of Archimedes and Aristotle, Copernicus claimed that, through careful observations and mathematical analysis, we could come to understand how the universe really worked, how its parts were really related to the whole. It was not enough to have mere hypothetical constructs which made it easier to understand the appearances. Furthermore, no single view of how the universe really works could dominate forever by the sheer force of having prevailed for a very long time.

If Copernicus was correct, Aristotle's physics was wrong, even though it had reigned for two thousand years. Further observations by Tycho Brahe and mathematical analysis of them by Johannes Kepler would strengthen this overthrow of Aristotle. A new way of thinking about the universe was emerging. Its full emergence, however, would be painful. Aristotelian natural philosophy had penetrated the whole fabric of the intellectual life of the West. Science could not be divorced from philosophy nor from theology. There was a certain unity to Aristotle's thought; if a part of it was wrong, the whole system was threatened. The birth pangs of modern science were just beginning to be felt.

Tensions Arise as Modern Science Is Born

There are several seminal tensions that are just beginning to take root at this early stage of the birth of modern science. They are healthy tensions which will continue to be nurtured up to our own day and will contribute to the vigor of the natural sciences. They are the kind of tensions which are common to us as human beings: the tension, for instance, in parenting between the tender loving care and discipline given to a child and the need to allow a maturing young person independence and a degree of self-determination; or the tension that each of us must maintain between an ordered, disciplined life with clear goals and the need to be open to the newness that each day brings and to be able to marvel and be surprised at all that comes to us spontaneously and unplanned. In all cases we must live with the tension and not destroy one or other of the alternatives.

At this epoch of the birth of modern science, one of the tensions is that between the attempt to show that our physical-mathematical models really represent reality, the drama that is being enacted in the universe, and the inability to obtain sufficient observations. The fundamental posture of an astronomer is to listen to the universe, to catch every possible photon of energy and seek to organize the information obtained. One problem is that the universe is very large compared to our smallness, and much of the universe we are seeking to understand is very distant. But even nearby objects can be quite opaque to our attempts to observe them accurately. One must be patient and accurate in collecting the information which comes to us from the universe.

One of the first clear examples of this is given by Kepler's use of the observations of Brahe to break through the age-old prejudice that heavenly bodies must move in circles. Brahe had assembled the best and most voluminous observations of the positions of the heavenly bodies ever seen up until his day. Kepler analyzed them and thus discovered that the planets are moving about the sun in elliptical orbits. The physical-mathematical model of Kepler both had its origins in Brahe's observations and also gave a unified explanation of them. But this did not cancel forever the tension between understanding and observing. As we shall see the universe is always, it seems, more subtle than we expect as it reveals itself to us through our observations. We will, centuries after Kepler and Brahe, find, for instance, that Mercury's elliptical orbit is not fixed in space-time, but that the orbit itself is precessing. Neither Kepler's laws nor Newton's universal gravity will be able to explain this. Ultimately, it will be explained by Einstein's relativity.

As in many aspects of life, a certain objective humility is required of the scientist who wishes to understand the universe. We must allow the universe to have its say and not try to force upon it our own unfounded theories. While mathematics may be considered the language of the universe, there are many subtleties which do not easily follow the logic of mathematics. The history of scientific discoveries has shown this. Every time that we develop a new technique of observing the universe we are surprised by what it tells us. When Galileo first lifted his rudimentary telescope and gazed from the window of his home in Padua at the Milky Way, he was overwhelmed by the sight of myriads of stars stretched out across the sky. His and our view of the universe was changed forever. The universe had spoken anew.

When Edwin Hubble first detected pulsating variable stars in the Andromeda nebula and determined that it was some twenty times further away than the size of our galaxy, we began to have the first inkling of the immensity of the universe. We were beginning to hear a completely new tale. When the first orbiting x-ray satellite was launched from Kenya and carried the name "Uhuru," which means freedom in Swahili, it discovered pulsating sources of x-rays, completely unknown and unpredicted objects. Again, the universe was speaking its mysteries. Eventually these came to be understood as some of the most tantalizing objects in the birth and death of stars, since they consist of two stars orbiting one another, one of which is a super-dense dead star and its companion a normal evolving star.

These are just a few examples of how fecund the universe is in its mysteries and of how attentive we must be, therefore, to find an opening to these mysteries by careful observations. It is jokingly said of some theoreticians that they did not want to be bothered with the facts. The facts cramp their style and do not let them roam freely with their pure ideas and pure mathematics. It surely is a joke, because theorists also realize that they must be humble before the fecundity of the universe. Hubris on the part of anyone who confronts the universe will inevitably lead to a complete inability to understand its mysteries.

This tension between theory and observations also receives an impetus, at times, from theory. Copernicus's improvement over Ptolemy by reducing the number of circular motions required to explain planetary motions was very much in the realm of theory, but it undoubtedly urged Kepler to find an even more simplifying explanation, elliptical orbits — this time, however, because he was faithful to the observations of Brahe.

This impetus from theory repeats itself in the history of scientific discoveries. Einstein was confronted with the necessity to add, in an inelegant manner, an ad hoc constant to his beautiful cosmological equations of general relativity because they required that, without that constant, the universe must be either expanding or contracting. At that time, there was no evidence that the universe was other than static; so theory had to conform to ignorance. When, more than a decade later, Hubble discovered from observations of distant galaxies that the universe is expanding, Einstein was humbled but also overjoyed. Theory had seen what was true before observations were available, but theory was hesitant, lacked self-confidence. Einstein had committed a folly in adding an ugly constant to his equations. He was so elated by Hubble's discovery that on a visit to California in 1931 he made a special trip to the top of Mt. Wilson, where Hubble had made the observations, to thank the great observational astronomer and to see at first hand the telescope which had shown that good theories can be correct, if you do not tinker with them.

We will see that there are other healthy tensions in the scientific search for understanding. Copernicus insisted — despite the attempts of Osiander with his preface to the *De Revolutionibus* to calm the controversies that were growing — that his theory was true in the sense that it corresponded to the real drama of the universe. But he had no observations that were convincing. The universe had not yet had its say. With Kepler's use of the observations of Brahe we have a listening station to the universe. Empirical evidence is becoming important, in fact, determinative of what is really real. We will see other tensions, not unlike those that all humans experience, as we proceed in our voyage to understand ourselves and the universe we inhabit.

Chapter Five

GALILEO AND THE BIRTH PANGS OF MODERN SCIENCE

THE HISTORY of the personal career of Galileo Galilei as a scientist has been, and continues to be, a fascinating one, a blend of tragedy and comedy in the richest, traditional sense of those terms. Born in Pisa in the same year as the birth of William Shakespeare and the death of Michelangelo Buonarotti, his life like theirs was to become bigger than life itself, a symbol of a critical stage in our freedom to search for ourselves in an evolving universe. But much more important and interesting to us — pilgrims who are searching for an understanding of our journey in the universe — is the role, not personal but public, that Galileo played in the inevitable march toward the birth of modern science from the beginnings with his immediate predecessors to the culmination with such figures as Newton, Leibniz, and Descartes.

It is very significant that Galileo, who was supported by his patrons, the Medicis, as a mathematician and admired by his colleagues under the same title, preferred to be known as a philosopher. He held the chair of mathematics both at Pisa and then at Padua. For Galileo and his contemporaries "natural philosophy" referred to the pursuit of a true understanding of the nature of the universe. Today we would call them "physicists." We will see that Galileo concretizes in his own life the tension we have spoken of previously between a hypothetical, mathematical explanation of the appearances and a model of what the universe is truly doing. Galileo's self-knowledge, his view of himself as a natural philosopher, will, as we shall see, prove to be of extreme significance in evaluating what he truly accomplished amid extreme adversity.

He first met opposition in 1589 when, upon taking up his teaching position at the University of Pisa, he began to challenge the Aristotelian notions of motion. The new professor of mathematics soon became an outsider among the Aristotelian philosophers of nature. Through his experiments he began to prove them wrong on every point. And in his teaching he relied heavily upon that of the Jesuits at the Roman College, some of whom were much more critical of Aristotle than any others throughout Europe. This climate of teaching and research in opposition to the majority suited Galileo perfectly. He loved opposition. At this time he even began suggesting that the earth rotated, an anathema to Aristotelians. Historians debate as to whether Galileo actually performed the experiment of dropping weights from the Leaning Tower of Pisa, but the experiment certainly is in keeping with his thinking. At this time, early in his career, Galileo was struggling with the contrast between a geocentric and heliocentric solar system and had not yet taken a firm position. Here we have the epitome of a scientist on his journey, as are we. Uncertain, but struggling to know the truth. And the truth would be known through experiments and observations. Modern science is being born.

But adversity was not always the dominant characteristic of Galileo's life. When he ended his teaching in Pisa, having created a bit of turmoil with his experiments to show that Aristotle's notion of motion was wrong, he obtained a position at the most prestigious university of its day, the University of Padua, where he spent, as he himself referred to it, "the happiest eighteen years of my life." The University of Padua is one of the oldest in Europe (probably dating to 1222), but what contributed principally to its renown in Galileo's time was its spirit of freedom in both research and teaching. This spirit, of course, suited Galileo quite well. During the early part of his eighteen years in Padua he seems to have oscillated back and forth in the strength of his adherence to Copernicanism.

The Way Is Not Always Straight and Narrow

It was during this time that he first came to the idea that the tides might provide strong evidence for the movement and rotation of the earth. In 1604 another "new star," like that observed by Tycho Brahe, suddenly appeared in the sky as bright as Jupiter, and Galileo courageously entered the great debate as to whether this "changing and corruptible" object lay in the distant realm of the heavens or was simply a phenomenon in the earth's atmosphere. One of the classical cornerstones of Aristotelian natural philosophy was again at stake. Galileo organized an observing campaign with colleagues in other European cites and from the combined observations was able to conclude that the object was very distant in the realm of the fixed stars. He was puzzled as to the nature of this object, whose position did not change, and he hesitated to publish anything as to its physical nature.

In his search for evidence in support of Copernicanism Galileo began to reason in another and quite clever way, a way which in the end proved futile. Claiming that the reason for the decrease in brightness of the new star must be its motion directly away from the earth, then if parallax could be observed this would necessarily mean that the observer (thus the earth) was moving, since it could not be due to the object moving across the observer's line of sight. Unfortunately, as before, no parallax could be measured. For this and other reasons Galileo undoubtedly harbored some misgivings about Copernicanism. Today we know what he, of course, could not know, that the object was a supernova in the galaxy, a rare event in terms of human observations of the heavens.

We might pause to reflect upon these experiences of Galileo in light of the growth toward modern science. Our scientific understanding of ourselves in the universe is never a simple straight and progressive path. It is rather like a spiral; we wander from one observation or experiment to the next, from one mathematical model to another and back and forth between observations, experiments, and mathematical analyses. Our hope is that in our meandering path we are, indeed, making progress, that we are coming closer to a true understanding of the way things are in the universe. This is precisely what Galileo was experiencing during his tranquil years of observations and reflection in Padua, and his experience has become an essential element in the birth of modern science. And we shall soon see that his further experiences will contribute even more to that development.

Somewhat disappointed in his search for direct proofs of Copernicanism, Galileo took up again his studies on motion begun in Pisa. These studies, especially those on the oscillations of a pendulum and those on falling bodies, which will come to full fruition only in the last years of his life with the publication in 1638 of his *Discourse on the Two New Sciences,* provided further arguments against the natural philosophy of Aristotle, and this indirectly contributed to the final acceptance of Copernicanism.

Little did Galileo expect, amid his meanderings from one experiment to the next and his growing conviction of the fundamental incorrectness of Aristotelian natural philosophy and his uncertainties about Copernicanism, what lay in store for him in the heavens. Toward the end of his long stay in Padua in 1609/10 he learned of the existence of an instrument, discovered almost certainly by a Dutchman, Hans Lippershey, which allowed one to see objects magnified and to large distances. He immediately sensed the possible usefulness of such an instrument for observing the heavens, and within a very short time he constructed the first of many telescopes for which he cleverly saw a commercial and military value, as well as scientific one. One of the reasons, perhaps, for his prominence in the history of science is that he had much greater success in the latter than in the former ventures. Who knows what would have happened had he successfully opened a shop for the sale of telescopes?

The Approach of Galileo to His Telescopic Observations

Before we turn our gaze upon Galileo with his perfected telescope pointed to the heavens, we would like to attempt to recover his state of mind at that moment. This is admittedly a very tendentious thing to do, but we think it is important to attempt to do so because what Galileo was doing holds great significance for understanding how modern science came to be. He was nearing the end of a relatively long, tranquil period of teaching and research, during which he had come to question at its roots the orthodox Aristotelian view of the known physical universe. But he had as yet no solid physical basis upon which to construct a replacement view. He sensed a unity in what he experienced in his studies of motion in the laboratory and what he saw in the heavens. But his view of the heavens was limited, although there was some expectation that — since with his telescope he had seen from Venice ships at sea at least ten times the distance at which they could be seen by the naked eye — he might go a bit beyond that limit.

He was uncertain about many things in the heavens. He had seen an object suddenly appear as bright as Jupiter and then slowly disappear; he had been able to conclude that it must be in the realm of the fixed stars, but he could venture nothing about its nature. Did he have expectations that with the telescope he would find out for certain whether the world was Copernican? Probably not. His expectations were not that specific. He simply knew that the small instrument he had worked hard to perfect, if he had already convinced his patrons of its value for military purposes, was surely of some value for scientific purposes. That in itself, although it may seem trite to us, was a major discovery. In brief, we propose to you a Galileo who was extremely curious, anxious to resolve some fundamental doubts, and clever enough to know that the instrument he held in his hands might contribute to settling those states of mind.

Obviously not everything happened in the first hours or even the first nights of observing. The vault of the heavens is vast and varied. It is difficult to reconstruct in any detail the progress of Galileo's observations; but from October 1609 through January 1610 there is every indication that he was absorbed in his telescopic observations. From his correspondence we learn that he had spent "the greater part of the winter nights under a peaceful open sky rather than in the warmth of his bedroom." They were obviously months of intense activity, not just at the telescope but also in his attempt to absorb and understand the significance of what he saw. His usual copious correspondence becomes significantly reduced during these months, but we do learn from it that he continued in his attempts to improve his telescope and even to introduce "some other invention." He finally succeeded in November of 1609 to make a telescope which magnified twenty times.

At times his emotional state breaks through in his correspondence. For Galileo these must have been the most exhilarating moments of his entire life. The observations will be carefully recorded in the *Sidereus Nuncius* but denuded for the most part, and by necessity, of their emotional content. What must have been, for instance, the state of mind of Galileo when for the first time he viewed the Milky Way in all of its splendor: innumerable stars resolved for the first time, splotches of light and darkness intertwined in an intriguing mosaic? He will actually say little about this of any scientific significance, and rightly so, since his observations had gone far beyond the capacity to understand. He could, nonetheless, be ignorant and still marvel.

But he will be very acute and intuitive when it comes to sensing the significance of his observations of the moon, of the phases of Venus, and, most of all, of the moons of Jupiter. The preconceptions of the Aristoteleans were crumbling before his eyes. He had remained silent long enough, over a three-month period, in his contemplations of the heavens. It was time to organize his thoughts and tell what he had seen and what he thought it meant. It was time to publish!

It happened quickly. The date of publication of the *Sidereus Nuncius* can be put at 1 March 1610, less than two months after his discovery of Jupiter's brightest moons and not more than five months after he had first pointed his telescope to the heavens. With this publication both science and the scientific view of the universe were forever changed, although Galileo would suffer much before this was realized. For the first time in over two thousand years new significant observational data had been put at the disposition of anyone who cared to think, not in abstract preconceptions but in obedience to what the universe had to say about itself. Modern science was aborning, and the birth pangs were already being felt. We know all too well how much Galileo suffered in that birth process.

Did Galileo's telescopic discoveries prove the Copernican system? Did Galileo himself think that they had so proven? There is no simple answer to these questions, since there is no simple definition of what one might mean by proof. Let us limit ourselves to asking whether, with all the information available to a contemporary of Galileo's, it was more reasonable to consider the earth as the center of the known universe or that there was some other center. The observation of at least one other center of motion, the clear evidence that at least some heavenly bodies were "corrupt," and most of all the immensity and density of the number of stars which populated the Milky Way left little doubt that the earth could no longer be reasonably considered the center of it all.

Of course, a more definitive conclusion will be possible in the coming centuries with the measurement of light aberration, of stellar parallaxes, and of the rotation of the Foucault pendulum. As to Galileo, his telescopic discoveries, presented in a booklet of fifty pages, the *Sidereus Nuncius,* will become the substance of his Copernican convictions lucidly presented in his *Dialogue on the Two Chief World Systems,* a work which he promised would appear "in a short while" but which actually appeared only twenty-two years later. His own convictions are clear, for instance, from his own statement in the *Dialogue:*

If we consider only the immense mass of the sphere of the stars in comparison to the smallness of the Earth's globe, which could be contained in the former many millions of times, and if furthermore we think upon the immense velocity required for that sphere to go around in the course of a night and a day, I cannot convince myself that anyone could be found who would consider it more reasonable and believable that the celestial sphere would be the one that is turning and that the globe would be at rest.

But Galileo was also wise enough to know that not everyone could be easily convinced. In a letter to Benedetto Castelli he wrote:

To convince the obstinate and those who care about nothing more than the vain applause of the most stupid and silly populace, the witness of the stars themselves would not be enough, even if they came down to the Earth to tell their own story.

While he could not bring the stars to earth, he had, with his telescope, taken the earth toward the stars, and he would spend the rest of his life drawing out the significance of those discoveries.

In reflecting upon these first telescopic observations of Galileo it is important to note the obvious uniqueness of astronomy among the natural sciences, at least ground-based astronomy, but also to a large extent space astronomy, in that it is observational and not experimental. The object being researched cannot be touched or managed. We can only look at it — nowadays, of course, with very sophisticated eyes — and try to understand it by applying what we know from scientific theory and from the experimental sciences. Galileo was the first true observational astronomer, but he was also an experimentalist. It is impressive, indeed, to visit the Istituto e Museo di Storia della Scienza in Florence, where one sees the many broken lenses from Galileo's attempts to make ever better telescopes. He himself stated that

> of the more than sixty telescopes made at great effort and expense I have been able to choose only a very small number ... which are apt to show all of the observations.

In that museum one also sees a display showing Galileo's application of the pendulum to a clock and his experiments with an inclined plane in search of the law of falling bodies. Before he pointed his finest telescope to the heavens, he had done his best to show experimentally that there were no serious "instrumental effects." Again, in his own words:

> Insofar as I can truthfully state it, during the infinite, or, better said, innumerable times that I have looked with this instrument I have never noticed any variation in its functioning and, therefore, I see that it always functions in the same way.

In fact, it was precisely through his dedication as an experimentalist, and in particular through his studies on motion, that he had come to have serious doubts about the Aristotelian concept of nature. What he sensed to be lacking was a true physics. The world models inherited from the Greeks were purely geometrical, and the geometry was based upon preconceived philosophical notions about the nature of objects in the universe: all objects had a natural place in the universe and consequently they had a natural motion. But there was no experimental justification for these preconceptions. They were simply based upon a philosophical idea of the degree of perfection of various objects.

But, in addition to his attachment to experiment and the sense for physics that derived from it, Galileo also nourished the idea that the true physical explanation of things must be simple in the richest meaning of that word. To be more specific, among several possible geometrical models the nature of the physical world would see to it that the simplest was the truest. For Galileo, the motion of falling bodies and the motion of the planets had something in common, and geometrical explanations were not sufficient. Physics was required.

The Fascination of Discovery

Let us pause for a moment to reflect, in the light of Galileo's telescopic discoveries, upon the very notion of discovery as a part of modern science. We might reflect upon three components contained in the notion of discovery: newness, an opening to the future, and, in the case of astronomical discovery, a blending of theory and observation. Discovery means that something new comes to light, and this generally happens suddenly and unexpectedly. While we cannot exclude that one can plan and even predict what is to be discovered, this is generally not the case. Galileo's telescopic discoveries surely brought us completely new and unexpected information about the universe. Taken as a whole that information was the first new significant observational data in over two thousand years, and it dramatically overturned the existing view of the universe.

It looked to the future. Were there other centers of motion such as seen with Jupiter and its moons? Did other planets like Venus show phases and changes in their apparent sizes? And what to make of those myriads of stars concentrated in that belt which crosses the sky and is intertwined with bright and dark clouds? All of these were questions for the future. Although neither Galileo nor any of his contemporaries had a well-developed comprehensive theory of the universe, Galileo clearly intuited that what he saw through his telescope was of profound significance. His discoveries were not limited to looking; they involved thinking. Henceforth no one could reasonably contemplate the universe in the tradition of Aristotle which had dominated thinking for over two millennia. A new theory was required.

In his thinking Galileo, as we have seen, was a self-proclaimed natural philosopher and was never actually inclined to be drawn into discussions of other matters alien to his principal interest. But should such other matters come to challenge, unjustifiably in his mind, the conclusions he attempted to draw from his observations, he would accept the challenge. Such was the case with his unwitting and, as it turns out, tragic entry into the field of theology. By his observational discoveries and his intuitive interpretation of them Galileo contributed significantly to the birth of modern science, whose first protagonist we have found in Kepler. But Galileo made as great, perhaps even a greater, contribution by his attitude of accepting the tentativeness of conclusions drawn from scientific reasoning and, therefore, an openness to revisions in light of further scientific evidence or of conclusions drawn from other sources of knowledge. For that reason he struggled valiantly to see that the Church did not declare itself definitively on scientific conclusions as long as they were tentative, even if they appeared to conflict with teachings of the Church. For him an appearance of conflict was not conflict and it could evanesce with further knowledge. Galileo was devoted to the Church; his life as well as his writings testify to this. In a letter written in 1615 before his troubles with the Church began he wrote:

> Whether in reaching such a decision it is advisable to consider, ponder, and examine what he [Copernicus] writes is something that I have done my best to show in an essay of mine. I hope the blessed God has granted me this, for I have no other aim but the honor of the Holy Church and do not direct my small labors to any other goal.

Science and Theology in Conflict

It was really against his wishes that Galileo was drawn into the controversy as to whether Copernicanism contradicted Holy Scripture. The Dominican Tommaso Caccini, in a sermon in the Church of Santa Maria Novella in Florence, first threw out the bait which drew Galileo into the Scripture controversy. In defending the literal sense of Scripture, Caccini said that all mathematicians practiced a diabolic art and disseminated heresies; this was especially true of the "Galileisti." This sermon had been preceded about a week before by a luncheon hosted by the Medicis at which, although Galileo was not present, his observations, especially those of the Medicean moons about Jupiter, were discussed. His friend Benedetto Castelli, who was present, wrote to let him know that, although all present believed his observations to be true, a discussion had arisen as to whether a moving earth contradicted Scripture.

Galileo became alarmed by these developments, since he wished the Church to make no pronouncements. So he wrote his first letter on these matters to Castelli, and sometime later he wrote an even more detailed letter to the Duchess Christina, who had been present at the lunch and had become disturbed by the possible heretical character of Copernicanism. In these letters Galileo essentially anticipated by about three centuries what the Catholic Church would come to teach concerning the interpretation of Scripture. But Galileo was not the Church, and he was proceeding to do precisely what the Council of Trent had recently condemned: he was privately interpreting Scripture. A Church under siege would soon react.

The scientific venture cannot be isolated from human affairs; nor should it be. On our journey to understand ourselves in the evolution of the universe we cannot ignore the multifaceted nature of our search. Galileo became increasingly aware of this, as did the Church. In this regard the views of Pope Urban VIII (Maffeo Barberini) and of Cardinal Robert Bellarmine are of interest. Urban VIII was convinced that no theory about the universe could claim to be other than a hypothesis, a way of explaining the appearances, because he held that God could have always made the universe in a different way and that we were not capable of fathoming the mind of

God. So no theory could claim to reveal the true nature of things. When, in a conversation with Galileo, he expressed this view, Galileo justly became alarmed. It was not difficult to recognize in this view a real death blow to the scientific venture, and in his *Dialogue* Galileo would place this view in the mouth of Simplicius, the Simpleton. Urban did not take kindly to that not so subtle attribution. While it cannot be said that Bellarmine held such an extreme view of science, it is difficult to know whether he ever accepted more than a hypothetical value to scientific theories. It appears not. What is clear is that he gave a primacy to the literal interpretation of Scripture when there was an apparent conflict with a scientific theory.

How do we wayfarers in our search to understand evaluate these opinions? If we are not convinced that what we are searching for is a true understanding of how the universe works, our venture is in vain. It is just one big game and not even a very entertaining one, since there is no challenge to measure what we think against what is. Furthermore, there should be no primacy of one way of knowing over another. As pilgrims on a search for understanding we must open our minds, and our hearts, to all possible sources of truth. When they apparently contradict one another, we must be open to an ultimate resolution. Galileo struggled for just this. In so doing he sought to find proofs for the Copernican system. He never claimed to have such final proofs; but he was convinced that he had suasive arguments in his telescope observations. Yes, Galileo was wrong in his argument from the tides; but the Church was wrong both in its reasons for condemning Galileo and in its excessive use of power against him.

The reasons offered for the condemnation were two-fold: in theology, Copernicanism contradicted Scripture as the Church understood it and as taught by the Fathers of the Church; in philosophy, Copernicanism contradicted Aristotle, whose philosophy was at the basis of the doctrinal teachings of the Church. In both cases history has proven this reasoning wrong. As to the excessive use of power, even if Galileo had disobeyed the injunction of 1616 not to hold that Copernicanism was true other than hypothetically, and there are many serious doubts about the contents of the injunction itself and of Galileo's adherence to it, to make him abjure as a heretic was an excessive use of power.

From the raw realities of history what we have seen is an all too human Church dealing with an all too human Galileo. This was a Church which would not recognize that the truth is not primarily to be possessed but to be sought after and treasured when it has in part been attained, and that truth is approached from many different disciplines and perspectives. From the history of science we have seen that progress in science cannot be divorced from the historical circumstances that surround it. As pilgrims in search of an understanding of ourselves in a universe in evolution we are standing with Galileo on the threshold of a new and exciting adventure in our journey. Many obstacles have been overcome: nature is not an illusion of dancing shadows nor is it dominated by magical and mysterious forces. There is a rationality to nature in our rudimentary understanding of it; its parts seem

to fit together into a whole. There are relationships between the parts, and we find that with mathematics we
can express those relationships accurately. There are laws
that govern, for instance, how the planets move about
the sun.

But there are factors which limit our freedom to think
as scientists; and one of the most powerful of these is
religion. Jealous, and with some reason, of what it holds
to be the truth given to it by God in the Holy Books, the
Church was wary of science and the growing success of
the march toward modern science. The condemnation of
Galileo is the unfortunate outcome which still haunts us
on our journey.

That haunting experience has some positive content
for us. It may lead us to ask the question: Did Galileo
sense that there was a personal force at work in the universe? What can we learn from his experience? Galileo
was a religious person. His faith in a personal God on
whom the universe depended was unshakable. As for all
of us, however, it was in specifying how God and the
universe were related that the challenge lay. Both from
a religious and a scientific point of view he could not
accept the reasoning of Pope Urban VIII, which we have
discussed above. For Galileo there was no arbitrariness in
the relationship of God to the universe. The universe for
Galileo had a rationality to it which reflected and imaged
the marvels of God himself. There was no taint of Platonism. The universe as a whole and the relationship among
all of its parts were real. Its rational structure could be
analyzed. The universe, in fact, was the Book of Nature,
revealing God to us in a way similar to the way God re-

vealed himself to us in the Sacred Books. As we had to learn how to read the Holy Books, witness Galileo's *Letter to the Duchess Christina,* so we must learn the language of the Book of Nature. We could thus come to an understanding of the universe and, therefore, of God reflected in the universe.

Galileo draws the logical conclusion from this way of thinking: the Book of Nature and the Book of Scriptures have one and the same author. They could not, therefore, be in conflict. This way of thinking about a religious dimension to the scientific enterprise will become ever more prominent as the birth of modern science reaches its climax in Isaac Newton. And then it will become so prominent in an increasingly rationalistic understanding of the universe that it will paradoxically turn to become a force for atheism in the growth of modern science.

Tensions between Traditions and New Discoveries

Galileo's experiences bring to light another healthy tension which asserts itself very definitively for him and is present down to our own day. We noted at the end of the last chapter the tension that exists between theory and observation in the search for an understanding of the universe. Now we note another tension: that between tradition and discovery.

None of us could exist, either physically or psychologically, without daily reference to our past roots. We are what we are today because of our ancestors, our cultural heritage, our knowledge of the past, an inherited language and way of thinking. We are to a great extent what those before us have been. But we are more. We are open to the future. What will happen to me the next moment and for all of my future is to some extent in my hands. Furthermore, there are the many mysteries of the universe and my place in it still to be discovered. Those discoveries are not necessarily contained implicitly in what is already known, only waiting to be uncovered. Before me there lies the vastness of the unknown. Wise explorers rely upon what has been handed on to them, but they must make their own way into the future. So it is with the scientific venture.

As he pursued his scientific venture, Galileo had to confront two traditions: that of the natural philosophy of Aristotle and that of the Church. The former was rooted in the centuries-old authority of a great philosopher; the latter in the authority of a powerful institution. As we have shown, he slowly but surely challenged the physics of the former by dint of observations and reasoning. The fundamental Aristotelian distinction between the heavenly and earthly realm and the natural places and motions of bodies began to crumble before the observations of spots on the sun and satellites orbiting Jupiter. We must remember, however, that Galileo never overcame the tradition of circular motion being required of heavenly bodies.

Traditions in which authority rests upon the intellectual prowess of former wise philosopher-scientists will slowly but inevitably give way to the newly attained knowledge and wisdom of successors. The history of scientific revolutions shows that a tension always exists between what is inherited and what is discovered.

Rarely is the past destroyed to make for the future. A good example of this is Einstein's relativity, which is in continuity with Newtonian gravity, but which it supersedes when we are dealing with large masses and large velocities.

Such, however, is not the case, at least as judged from Galileo's history, when the traditions at stake are under the authority of the Church. Here the question is much more complicated, since we are dealing with truths which are protected by an institution and, in this case, a powerful one. Let us examine this tension in the specific case of Galileo, since it will shed a great deal of light on the respective roles of science and religious belief in our search for understanding.

Galileo was accused by the Congregation of the Holy Office in 1633 of not having obeyed a Church decree of 1616 which said that Copernicanism could be taught only as an hypothesis. Even in recent times it is said of him that he made no distinction between the scientific approach to natural phenomena and a reflection on nature of the philosophical order, and so he rejected the judgment that Copernicanism was a hypothesis, since it had not been confirmed by irrefutable proofs.

Much could be said about this characterization of the scientific method and Galileo's use of it. There is an ambiguity involved in the use of the word "hypothesis." There are two distinctly different uses of the word: a mathematical expedient to predict celestial events or an attempt to understand the true nature of the heavens. This important difference in meaning must be seen against the history of the word's use from antiquity through medieval Christianity to the time of Copernicus through to Galileo. As we have seen, in his attempt to save Copernicus, Osiander, unbeknownst to the author and contrary to his intent, wrote his famous preface to advise the reader that the *De Revolutionibus* was intended in the tradition of medieval astronomy only in the former sense, a mathematical expedient. There is no doubt that Galileo understood his own investigations to be an attempt to understand the true nature of things. It is well known that he preferred to be known as a philosopher of nature instead of a mathematician. It can be debated as to whether Galileo himself was ever convinced that he had irrefutable proofs for Copernicanism (involved in that debate would be the very meaning of proof for him), but it cannot be denied that he sought evidence to show that Copernicanism was really true and not just a mathematical expedient. Galileo rejected that Copernicanism was a hypothesis in the former sense. He sought to find experimental verification of it in the latter sense.

The Church has recently described the whole affair as a "tragic mutual incomprehension." Galileo's incomprehension is said to be what has been described above, an ambiguous accusation at best. As to the incomprehension on the part of the Church, fault is placed exclusively on theologians, most of whom did not know how to examine their own criteria of Scriptural interpretation in light of the new science. Thus they unduly transposed a question of factual observation into the realm of faith.

This leads us to ask whether the fundamental epistemic differences between science and faith have been adequately understood. The Galileo case presents a specific opportunity to come to understand the relationship of contemporary scientific culture and inherited religious culture. Could the contrast between authority in the Church and authority in science give rise to another modern Galileo affair? In the Catholic tradition there is what has been called a "logic of centralized authority," required by the fact that revelation is derived from Scripture, which is officially interpreted only by the Church. In contrast, authority in science is essentially derived from empirical evidence, which is the ultimate criterion of the veracity of scientific theory. In the case of Galileo the defendant is a scientific idea and the authority which condemns that idea derives from the decree of the Council of Trent on the interpretation of Scripture.

What would have been the consequences if, instead of exercising its authority in this case, the Church had suspended judgment? But, having already exercised that authority over a scientific idea, the Church then applied that authority in a personal injunction given to Galileo. There is a clear distinction here between authority exercised over the intellectual content of a scientific idea and that exercised over a person in the enforcement of the former. This results in the fact that the abjuration forced on Galileo in 1633 was intended to break his will rather than his reason. The tension between tradition and discovery in the scientific venture has many consequences, not least of which is respect for the freedom of responsible individuals to seek the truth.

~ *Chapter Six* ~

THE AGE OF RATIONALISM: PRINCIPAL PROTAGONISTS, DESCARTES AND NEWTON

WE HAVE ARRIVED at a critical point in our journey. The groundwork has been laid for the birth of modern science; but we still await a synthesis, an insight which will unify past discoveries and launch us along our path to the future. As before, we cannot speak of every scientist who contributed to this synthesis, so we select two of the chief protagonists, Descartes and Newton.

Descartes: A Path Downward from Pure Geometry to the World of the Senses

In Descartes we find a unique approach to the attempt to understand ourselves in the evolving universe. By mastering first principles with clear, distinct, and fundamental ideas he felt he could descend to an understanding of all of the phenomena of nature. The key direction is "descent." At the risk of oversimplifying his thought, we can say that for Descartes the understanding of nature was a one-way street; one proceeded from clear concepts to explain the causes of all things. And the most important of these concepts were those derived from geometry.

It is curious that the first work that Descartes wrote, although it was published after his death, was on music, *Compendium Musicae*. Do we have here an echo of the Pythagoreans and of Kepler's *Harmony of the Spheres*? Do we have an intimation of Platonism, a cave of shadows of an ideal world of geometrical figures? Indeed, Descartes invented the field of analytical geometry and made a great contribution to the role of mathematics in modern physics. On the other hand he introduced a radical dualism into the understanding of nature: for him matter was simply extended substance which had been given motion at creation, and mind was unextended thinking substance. We will see that this tension between matter and mind will grow increasingly as we continue on our journey. Descartes posed a challenge by, in simple words, denying the tension. And yet we wayfarers, beings in equilibrium between matter and spirit, experience the tension in each moment of our lives.

For Descartes dualistic thinking led him to consider the material universe as nothing but matter in motion. Thus, all science was simply mechanics. This applied to animals as well as to the human body. He was about to publish a treatise on these topics when he learned of Galileo's condemnation in 1633, and he decided to withhold publication. Prudence is the better part of valor! Descartes treatise, *L'homme,* was published only after his death when neither valor nor prudence were of much use to him.

In practice, however, Descartes was not always completely consistent with the philosophy just elucidated. Few of us are completely consistent! He wrote, for instance, in the *Discours:* "I notice also with respect to experiments that they become so much the more necessary, the more we advance in knowledge." He expressed criticism in his *Rules* "of those philosophers who neglect experiments and expect truth to rise from their own heads like Minerva from Jupiter's." He himself spent a great deal of time in experimental observation. He dissected and vivisected embryos of birds and cattle and dissected dogs, cats, rabbits, and cod. He carefully observed the rainbow and other optical phenomena.

Despite his emphasis upon the descent from clear ideas to the phenomena of nature he was also insistent that experiment and observation alone could show whether the clear ideas (models) corresponded to reality. And so, although he is judged by history to have given excessive weight to the "clear ideas" and thus was a precursor of rationalism, there was in practice a tension in his judgment of the weight of the inductive method, of the importance of observation and experimentation in evaluating our "clear ideas."

Our evaluation of Descartes as a pilgrim like us should not concentrate upon whether his answers were correct but rather upon whether the questions he posed, as to the methods by which we are to understand ourselves in the universe, were fruitful. Did they sustain us and push us forward in our journey? The stance of Descartes was thoroughly optimistic. If we could know the "clear ideas" we would know all of nature. Optimistic tendencies such as this will continue to arise as our pilgrimage progresses. They are like bright rays of sunshine suddenly breaking through the dark clouds which obscure our complex and confused journey. There is, for instance, a fond hope that scientists will someday soon arrive at a unification of the four fundamental forces at work in the universe and at a cosmology which will provide us with the so-called "Theory of Everything." But we will return to these ideas later. Let us now continue on our journey, having been refreshed by Descartes's optimistic rationalism, even though we may be a bit dubious of its validity.

Newton and the Unification of Scientific Knowledge

With Newton we come to the first great synthesis in modern science. The results obtained by his renowned immediate predecessors, such as Galileo and Kepler, will be brought together and unified in a simple universal explanation. Newton was born almost exactly one year after Galileo's death. We know that Newton read Galileo's *Sidereus Nuncius* and his *Dialogue* and Kepler's *Dioptrice* and *Astronomia Nova*. His familiarity with what had been accomplished by scientists during the century before his birth was a stimulus to his own thinking. In his writings, principally in the *Philosophiae Naturalis Principia Mathematica* and in *Opticks*, Newton conveys the impression that he is following a strict, logical, deductive train of reasoning to arrive at clear and certain conclusions.

He was profoundly impressed by the implications for Copernicanism of the observations reported by Galileo in his *Sidereus Nuncius*. In reality it was by intuition and insight that he was able to leap forward in an under- standing of the universe. He himself admitted that it was the falling apple which initiated his musings which led eventually to the formulation of the universal law of gravity. His intuitive leap required, of course, a deliberate retreat to establish the logical steps which justified the leap. By combining Kepler's third law, which related the period of a planet's revolution about the sun to its mean distance from the sun, with the law of centrifugal force, he derived algebraically the inverse square distance law for gravity.

If the law of gravity was universal, it applied to the moon as well as to the famous apple. So why not do a simple calculation, said Newton to himself? It required two simple assumptions: that the total mass of the earth can be considered to be a point mass at the center of the earth and that the earth and the moon were an isolated system. The second assumption is obviously not true, but why not see how far from the truth it is? This is called a simplifying assumption, a methodological cornerstone of modern science. The first assumption will be shown later on to be exactly true mathematically. From his cal- culations of the acceleration of the moon and that of the apple Newton, in his own words, "found them to answer pretty nearly." We do not know quantitatively what he meant by "nearly," but we do know that his ratio for the radius of the earth to the moon's distance differed from the modern value by only three ten thousandths.

For some unknown reason Newton delayed for twenty year's the announcement of his discovery. Some think that his calculation in the "moon test" did not give adequate agreement for the acceleration of the moon and of the apple and that he, therefore, sought an additional force to gravity. Others say that, since it was only in 1685 that he proved the law for the attraction by a sphere, he doubted the validity of his first assumption. At any rate, although the true reason for Newton's delay in announcing his discovery is not known, we have here an opportunity to reflect upon the delicate interplay in scientific discovery of intuition, assumptions, observations, quantitative calculations, and evaluation of the results of predecessors. We are witnessing here the birth of modern science, and, while in the end we may characterize it as rationalism, it is important to note the many ingredients that contribute to the final product. The path to discovery is never a straight and narrow one. Hesitancy and, at times, the combination of seemingly contradictory aspects of reality play an important role.

An exemplary case of the later is seen in Newton's attempts to understand the nature of light. He is often presented as the classical proponent in the seventeenth century of the corpuscular nature of light. Indeed, he sought a universality in nature by embracing the corpuscular theory of light because then he could more easily analyze it as he did gross bodies by the forces acting upon it. And yet in that very analysis he hinted at another nature to light. He claimed that the refraction and reflection of rays of light could best be understood if light consisted of small bodies which through attraction or a force like it stirred up oscillations in the medium in which they traveled. The key word here is, of course, oscillations, and, although we are a long way from the wave theory of light, there are surely intimations of it.

In his voluminous treatise on light, *Opticks,* in Book II he discusses in detail what were later called "Newton's rings," interference patterns which in the course of history could only be adequately explained by the wave nature of light. We now know that light is both a wave and a corpuscle, or particle. Newton surely had an intimation of this, and yet in his struggle to universalize and simplify the laws of physics he favored the corpuscular nature of light. We see here that even the application of the most fundamental criteria for the veracity of a given scientific model is difficult and not without its treacherous enticements to error.

Let us return to another interesting part of the history of Newton's discovery of the law of gravity. When Robert Hooke became secretary of the British Royal Society, he invited Newton to engage in a private philosophical correspondence. Hooke initiated the exchange by asking Newton's comments on his analysis of the motion of a body under a central force field. In reply Newton all but ignored Hooke's suggestion and went on to describe what he called a "fancy of my own about discovering the earth's diurnal motion, a spiral path that a free-falling body would follow as it supposedly fell to earth." Hooke responded that the path would not be a spiral but an ellipse. In his response Newton agreed that it would not be a spiral, but he was hesitant to accept that it would be an ellipse. Hooke was insistent and kept pressuring Newton.

Thanks to Hooke's insistence Newton came to realize the significance of Kepler's second law: as planets orbit the sun they sweep out equal areas in equal units of time. By using the method of limits and of infinitesimals (today's differential calculus) Newton showed that, if the area law of Kepler holds, the elliptical shape of an orbit implies that any force directed to a focus must vary inversely as the square of the distance. Furthermore, he showed that the area law is a necessary and sufficient condition that the force on a moving body be directed to the center. Thus, for the first time the true significance of Kepler's laws of planetary motion was revealed: the area condition was equivalent to the action of a central force and the occurrence of an ellipse required an inverse square force field. Copernicus's hypothesis, Galileo's observations of Jupiter's Medicean satellites and his treatment of falling bodies, and Kepler's laws could eventually all be explained by gravity.

But there is a sense in which Newton's unification also modified the results of his predecessors. Kepler's laws strictly applied only to a point mass moving about a mathematical center of force and with no other stationary or moving masses present. Such a situation is a mere hypothesis, but a very useful one for studying the real world. Furthermore, Newton showed the rate of free fall of bodies is not constant, as Galileo asserted, but varies with distance from the center of the earth and with latitude on the earth's surface.

Hooke's insistence with Newton, although Hooke had made mathematical errors in his own analysis, appears to have been critical to Newton's discovery. Science seldom, if ever, advances by scientists acting in benign isolation. Human interactions, friendly or otherwise, are almost always necessary as a stimulus to scientific discovery. The journey to an understanding of the universe is a social phenomenon. It is in sharing and dialogue that we proceed along the path to further discovery.

An Exaggerated Rationalism

In the second edition of his *Philosophiae Naturalis Principia Mathematica* Newton added what has become his famous *Scholium Generale,* in which he stated that "it is not to be conceived that mere mechanical causes could give birth to so many regular motions" and then went on to speak of God "to discourse of whom from phenomena does certainly belong to Natural Philosophy." Like many of his contemporaries Newton believed that scientific investigation would provide proofs for the existence of God in the regularities of nature. We must now examine more carefully this claim and its consequences for the future of our journey.

It was paradoxically precisely this attempt by Newton and others in the seventeenth and eighteenth centuries to establish a rational basis for religious belief through arguments derived from philosophy and the natural sciences that led to the corruption of religious belief. Religion yielded to the temptation to root its own existence in the rational certitudes characteristic of the natural sciences. It was thought that the existence of God must be so well established from philosophical arguments that evidence derived from religious experience itself became secondary or even forgotten. This rationalist tendency found its apex in the enlistment of the new science, characterized by such figures as Newton and Descartes, to provide the foundation for religion.

Newton, for instance, attempted to prove the existence of God by the fact that the universe did not collapse. He, indeed, knew his law of gravity very well and that it would inevitably cause a finite static distribution of material, which is what he thought the universe to be, to collapse to a central mass. But he did not know the universe as we know it today, a dynamic, expanding, and evolving one. We shall see this shortly. When such proofs as Newton's for God's existence failed, as they always and inevitably must, in the minds of many God himself disappeared. The origins of modern disbelief lie in that attempt to use God as the explanation of scientific phenomena. Science, at its very roots, had tempted religion to embrace its own kind of rationalism, and those roots are still sprouting flourishing, green shoots of excessive use of reason in religious belief.

To summarize, modern science has its origins in the development of the experimental method in the twelfth and thirteenth centuries. In the seventeenth century, with Galileo as a principal protagonist, the experimental method was perfected and the application of mathematics to scientific research was begun. With Newton we come to the real beginning of modern science. Although the Galileo case, as it is called, provides the classical example of confrontation between science and religion, it is really in the misappropriation of modern science by such as Newton to mistakenly establish the foundations

for religious belief that we find the roots of a much
more deep-seated confrontation. From these roots, in
fact, sprung the divorce between science and religion.
Thus science served as a temptress to religion. The certainties born of the scientific method gave birth to the
desire for identical certainties as a foundation for religious belief. That desire was radically misplaced and led
to a lengthy period of misunderstanding between religion
and science.

As an inheritance from these developments of the seventeenth and eighteenth centuries there has been within
the Churches a tendency to associate scientific research
with atheism. Up until several decades ago, for instance,
all of the organization of formal dialogue between the
Catholic Church and the world of science was handled by
the Vatican Secretariat for Non-believers (currently called
the Pontifical Council for Dialogue with Non-believers).
Much of that dialogue is now organized by the Pontifical
Council for Culture, founded in 1982.

Thus came about the suspicion of science as a threat
to religious belief, and we are we still tainted with it.
Of course there have been historical incidents, Giordano
Bruno, Galileo, Darwin, Teilhard de Chardin, some various descendants of Aristotle including Aquinas, in which
the official Church and scientists engaged in battles, at
times rather bitter ones. But why should we universalize
from these incidents to create what John Paul II in the
case of Galileo called "a myth." We do not universalize
from the history of the Borgia popes that moral turpitude
is associated with the papacy. We no longer universalize
from the history of usury in the Middle Ages that banks

are by their nature corrupt. Why do the Churches still have a suspicion of science?

A fundamental problem with all of the attempts to use the rational processes of science to either assert or deny the existence of God or to limit his action is that they primarily view God as Explanation. We know from Scripture and from tradition that God revealed himself as one who pours out himself in love and not as one who explains things. God is primarily LOVE. We shall soon have an opportunity to pursue further these reflections.

The Universe in Our Heads

But let us return to a more positive view of what is occurring on our pilgrimage. An amazing thing was happening in the seventeenth and eighteenth centuries. We were beginning to develop methods whereby we could put the universe in our heads. Of course, we cannot take this literally, but, nonetheless, we have become so accustomed to what occurred that we have ceased to marvel at this magnificent happening. By using mathematical physics we were able to analyze the universe and come to at least some modest understanding of it. We pilgrims must pause for a moment to appreciate what was happening. We were developing methods whereby we would eventually extend our knowledge to objects that were trillions of times further away than the extent of our outstretched arms. Astrophysics is a unique science. We cannot perform experiments on the objects we seek to understand. We can only let them speak to us from their distant abodes in the universe. We must tune ourselves to understand those signals that have been traveling through the universe for billions of years. In us the universe has become self-reflective. It has a consciousness of itself and is in travail to mature in its self-understanding.

At this crucial moment when mathematics and physics are maturing to the point of becoming the essential ingredients of the sciences, we note an increasing tension, concretized in the persons of Descartes and Newton but already noted many times before, between what we might in simple terms describe as the downward and upward movements in our knowledge of the universe and ourselves in it. Do we come to a true understanding by starting, like Plato and Descartes, with clear and certain ideas, an eternal, preexisting, immutable, rational structure of all that exists? And do we then seek to find the revelation of this world of ideas in the adulterated concreteness of the visible universe to which we are consigned to wander in search of who we are in this seemingly complex and complicated agglomeration of concrete particular beings? Or is there a rational structure imbedded in the universe which we see and touch and breathe? Were the apple on Newton's head and his knowledge of Galileo's observations of Jupiter's satellites necessary for him to have come to the discovery of the universal law of gravity? There appears to be no definitive answer to this question, and, perhaps, the very posing of the question is somewhat inaccurate and tendentious. And yet we sense a kind of unavoidable impulse to ask it, because we feel within ourselves this same tension between ideas and lived experiences. We seek to unify and bring meaning to all that we experience in our journey in the universe. And this tension seems to be present in all of our experiences, especially in those which we call religious.

Christianity Says the Universe Has Meaning

As we have described at the beginning of our journey, our ancestors sought to explain what they experienced by associating gods with the forces of nature. The Greek philosophers began to seek explanations in the orderly structure of lived experiences. But they could not resolve the question as to where that orderly, rational structure actually resided: in the world of eternal ideas, in the realm of their gods, or in the world in which they lived.

In parallel with these diverse ways of thinking, religious experiences were becoming more structured and institutionalized, evolving into what are today the world's major religions. These identifiable religious institutions, such as Islam, Buddhism, Judaism, and Christianity, differ among themselves as to the relative emphasis they place on the two sides of the tension described above, between the "downward" and the "upward." All of the world's major religions are revealed, i.e., they lay claim to having received from elsewhere the content of their beliefs. The Judaeo-Christian religious tradition has emphasized from its very beginnings the workings of God in human history. God speaks in human beings chosen by him, the patriarchs and the prophets, and he also speaks in a burning bush, in water from a rock, and eventually in his own Son, who, having abided eternally with the

Father, at a certain moment in human history becomes man. This is the assertion of religious faith.

Early Christian reflection upon these lived, historical events, especially those recorded in St. John's Gospel, sees in them the insertion of God's plan, thought, word (St. John uses the word *logos*, inherited from the Greeks) into our universe. "The Word of God became flesh." This revelation, which the Judaeo-Christian tradition believes is spoken by God through his chosen spokespersons, has enormous consequences for assuaging the tension between the "downward" and "upward" we have described in our scientific knowledge of the universe. There are surely similarities in the tension present in both the religious and scientific experiences. The Judaeo-Christian experience affirms emphatically the enfleshment of the divine, and, since God is the source of the meaning of all things, that meaning too becomes incarnate.

Some see in this religious belief the foundations of modern science. A rigorous attempt to observe the universe in a systematic way and to analyze those observations by rational processes, principally using mathematics, will be rewarded with understanding because the rational structure is there in the universe to be discovered by human ingenuity. Since God has come among us in his Son, we can discover the meaning of the universe, or at least it is worth the struggle to do so, by living intelligently in the universe. Religious experience thus provides the inspiration for scientific investigation.

What are we to make of these assertions? Have we succumbed to a too facile assimilation of religious and scientific experiences? Or, on the other hand, is there truly at the origins of modern science the religious inspiration that God and his plan for the universe are incarnate? At a minimum, these two experiences are not incompatible; and the history of religions and of the origins of modern science certainly appear to support the connection we have presented.

This, however, makes ever more poignant the temptation which we have already addressed, namely, that religious belief be led astray to seek the same rational certitudes that we strive to obtain in the natural sciences. While religious belief may have played a key role in the inspiration of modern science, we now know that religious experience cannot be limited to that which science can discover. To use the concepts coined by Galileo, both the Book of Nature and the Book of Sacred Scripture can be sources of coming to know God's love incarnate in the universe. We might extend the Book of Scripture to include all that is contained in the lived experience of the believing community.

But knowing God's love through rational means is not sufficient; his love must be experienced. Such experience of God exceeds the content of the Book of Nature, just as any author is much more than what he or she can put into a book. Such experience also exceeds the Book of Scripture, taken even in the broader sense, if we approach the Book of Scripture only as an exercise in reason. From our experience as wanderers in the universe we know that there are many ways whereby we come to know the universe and ourselves as part of it. To seize upon one experience to the exclusion of others or to confuse them by failing to realize their diversity is a betrayal of all experience. While religious experience in the Judaeo-Christian tradition may have inspired the birth of the rational process peculiar to the natural sciences, it is mistaken to assume that rational processes exhaust the primordial experience of God, the source of both the Book of Nature and the Book of Scripture.

~ *Chapter Seven* ~

THE STARS
LOOK DOWN ON US

W E HAVE REFLECTED upon the ancients' view of the heavens and upon the birth of modern science. Let us now take our first glimpse of modern science as we attempt to understand the stars. This will lead us once more to reflect upon our place in this vast universe of stars and galaxies and to appreciate how much we are a part of it all.

What Is a Star?

As we view the star-filled heavens we are overwhelmed by the immensity of it all. We are also inevitably drawn to ask: what is a star? We have come a long way since our distant ancestors viewed essentially the same heavens. They had a different approach than we do today. Our ancestors saw themselves as detached from the universe. For instance, at Stonehenge on the Salisbury Plains of current-day England they created at about the time of the Prophet Abraham a monument which is now known to have had a twofold purpose. It was a place of worship where they offered sacrifices to their gods. At the same time, it was an astronomical observatory where they studied the movements of the heavenly bodies.

But these studies were related to their immediate needs. When should they plant? When would they reap? How could they predict the average variations in temperature during the year? How long was the year? Their astronomy was practical because they had come to realize that, in addition to placating the gods who determined their fate, they also had to work to win their own good fortune. Where were their gods and heroes? They were up in the sky, like Orion the Hunter. They lived in a distinct physical world. When we look today with infrared sensors at this same constellation, we see that it is teeming with newborn stars. And, as we shall soon see, we have been born of those stars. It took three generations of stars to provide the chemicals in the universe to form a human being. We are made of stardust. And so, when we ask the question, What is a star? we are asking a question about ourselves.

As we have seen, Galileo was the first to use a telescope to view the heavens in a search to understand what he saw. And when from his home in Padua he viewed the Milky Way, he saw that it was not a hazy swath of clouds but rather a swarm of billions and billions of stars. We now know that what he saw was simply a small part of our galaxy, an immense array of some 200 billion stars with spiral arms in which stars are born. It measures across 100 million light years. When we look out further in the universe beyond our Milky Way we see other galaxies, many of them spiral like our own. We shall speak of all of this in the next chapter. Let us return now to our question: what is a star? It should never cease to make us marvel that, with the modern tools of astrophysics, we can come to a conclusive answer to that question.

Each star is but a point of light. (In addition to that of the sun only a few other stars have had their surfaces resolved by special techniques.) We gather that light today by large, sophisticated telescopes and auxiliary instruments, and by analyzing that light with the use of mathematical physics we come to know what a star is made of, how it came to be, its age, its life history, its mass, motion, etc.

Only after many centuries did our ancestors come to distinguish what are truly stars from the many other bright objects in the sky. They noted, for instance, that some of those bright objects wandered back and forth against the pattern of fixed stars. These stars were nomads or wanderers, just like many of those who observed them, and so they were named "planets" from the Greek word for wanderer. Today we know that they are but chunks of material orbiting a star we call the sun. But, what is a star? It is a ball of gas, mostly hydrogen, which is so condensed and, therefore, so hot in its interior that it has ignited a thermonuclear furnace which supplies the energy by which it shines. But how do we know this? This question becomes ever more pressing when we realize that the lifetime of a star like the sun is 100 million times a human lifetime and that the light from even the nearest star to the sun takes about five years and from the nearest galaxy 2 million years to reach us. How have we come to know so much about these objects, considering that we live for so short a time compared to the duration of their existence and that they are so distant?

The answer is a very direct one. We discover what stars are by understanding what light is and the messages that it contains for us, since light from the stars is our only source of information about them. The most obvious fact about the light from stars is that it comes in different colors. Some stars are very blue, some very red. We have come to know by theoretical and experimental studies of gases in laboratories, the stars being bundles of gas, that the different colors are an indication of the different surface temperatures of the stars. A blue star may be four to five times hotter and a red star three times cooler than the sun. In order to make these determinations we must, of course, measure the color of a star's light very carefully. We do this by studying the spectrum of the light by, for instance, dispersing it through a prism. When we do this we also note that there are characteristic sets of lines in the spectrum due also, for the most part, to the surface temperature.

After the observation of many stars in this way it became clear that certain patterns of lines repeated themselves and that it was possible to classify stars according to their spectra. These spectral classes then became a powerful tool for the study of a star's life history. A fascinating empirical relationship was discovered at the beginning of the twentieth century between the spectral type of a star and its intrinsic brightness. If, for instance, for a cluster of hundreds of stars we plot the brightness versus the spectral type for each star we find that the points plotted follow a sequence, descending diagonally from the brightest, bluest stars to the faintest, reddest stars. Furthermore, the exact configuration in this brightness-spectral type plot varies with different clusters of stars. By using mathematical physics we have been able to understand these differences as due to the various ages of the clusters.

Let us follow intuitively the more vigorous reasoning supplied by mathematical physics. A cluster consists of a family of stars of different masses, formed from various pieces resulting from the breakup of a large gaseous cloud. Due to gravity each piece began to collapse and, consequently, to heat up until the internal temperature was sufficiently high to start a thermonuclear furnace by converting hydrogen to helium. At this point we have a star. More massive stars collapse more rapidly, reaching a higher internal temperature, and so their thermonuclear furnace is more energetic. They are bright, blue stars. The less massive stars collapse more slowly, reach a lower internal temperature, and so are less energetic. They are faint, red stars. The sun happens to be intermediate, a yellow-green star with a surface temperature of about 6,500 degrees Kelvin (absolute zero scale). Of course, the more massive stars will burn up their thermonuclear fuel more rapidly and so will "die" sooner than the less massive stars. Thus, we see intuitively that the life and death of stars are determined by their mass.

We have referred several times to the thermonuclear furnace in the nucleus of a star. In fact, this is precisely what makes a star; it is the source of all of the star's energy, and when it ceases to function, the star, as we have seen, dies. It was only, however, at the beginning of the twentieth century that scientists began to get some grasp of what makes a star shine. The challenge, in fact, came not from astronomy, from studying the stars, but from studies of the earth. Biologists, geologists, and paleontologists found, from several independent sources of evidence, that the earth must be at least several billion years old. This age implies that the sun must be at least as old, since the paleontological evidence required that the energy from the sun must have been present on the earth in about the same amount as it is today. But there was no source known that could provide the enormous amount of energy supplied by the sun over billions of years. For instance, fossil fuels of the total mass of the sun would supply such energy for only about five thousand years.

In 1905 with his special theory of relativity Einstein showed that mass and energy were convertible. Since by his theory the conversion of mass to energy was by the square of the velocity of light (a very large number), a small amount of mass could provide enormous amounts of energy. Could this be the source of solar and stellar energy? In the 1920s the British astronomer Sir Arthur Stanley Eddington, through his studies of stellar structure, speculated that the internal temperature of a star like the sun would be millions of degrees. He was correct, and today we know that this is sufficient to cause hydrogen nuclei to fuse into helium nuclei, with a loss of mass equivalent to that of an electron. This was exactly what Einstein had theorized, the conversion of a small amount of mass into great amounts of energy. It is now known that such fusion processes are the source of almost all stellar energy.

It is interesting to note that scientists were driven to

an understanding of stellar interiors and the sources of stellar energy by conclusions drawn from studies of the earth. We should also pause to note the way in which we have come to an understanding of a star's life and death and the consequences of that understanding. First we make observations of two fundamental parameters: brightness and spectral type. Then we become aware, in a rather fortuitous way, of a relationship between these parameters. The empirical relationship is so striking that we are urged on to try to understand it. Through the use of what we know from mathematical physics we succeed in coming to an understanding of the birth and death of stars.

Why does a star die? As it converts hydrogen to helium in its core, a star succeeds by the radiant energy generated to keep its outer layers from crushing in as gravity will inevitably cause them to do. Radiation pressure is warring against gravity to keep the star "alive." An equilibrium is established between the two. But eventually, and for massive stars more rapidly, the thermonuclear fuel is exhausted. There are intermediate stages, depending on the star's mass, of the conversion of helium to carbon, to nitrogen to oxygen, all the way up the periodic table to iron, but finally for every star there comes the "end of the line." This end is due to the fact that the conversion of iron to even heavier elements requires that the star eat up energy. And to live the star needs to create energy.

This is the struggle to survive on a cosmic scale. The star can no longer generate enough energy in its core to withstand the infall of its outer shells, and it collapses for

a last time, expelling its outer shells of material. It becomes a superdense object, like a white dwarf, a neutron
star, or a black hole, and can generate no more energy.
It shines for some time by gravitational energy stored up
from its collapse, but it will soon dissipate all of that energy to become a dead piece of nonradiating mass in the
universe. If we compare the lifetime of a star like the sun
to our own lifetime, it is curious to note that, although
it took about 20 million years for the sun to be born, it
is actually born five times faster than we are, if we judge
birthrate by total lifetime. We are born in about one hundredth of our lifetime. The sun is now about 5 billion
years old and has enough thermonuclear fuel to go on
for another 5 billion years. So the sun was born in one
five-hundredth of its lifetime!

We note that with each generation of stars the chemical elements in the universe are being transformed from
the lighter to the heavier elements. The original hydrogen
of the universe is being converted in the thermonuclear
furnace of stars to helium and then to carbon, to nitrogen, to oxygen, and finally to iron. And except for a bit of
helium and some lighter elements made in the early hot
universe, the birth and death of stars is the only means
available to get the heavier elements. We are, of course,
made of these heavier elements, and so we can claim to
be made of stardust.

Stars Provide the Elements of Life

We find here a interplay between the living and nonliving
universe which may be of interest to us in our attempt

to understand our wanderings in the universe. In a constantly cooling universe, because it was expanding, there would have been no human beings had there been no development of hot spots where the chemistry for life could be made through thermonuclear reactions. No stars, no life! This intimate relationship, established scientifically, poses obvious questions for that part of life, ourselves included, which has become intelligent, auto-reflective, and capable of asking questions such as the following. Could there be a universe with no stars? There is no scientific reason to deny that possibility. If there were no stars, could there still be life? There is no scientific reason to suggest that there could be. Did the universe make stars in order to make life? This is a question which certainly goes beyond the bounds of science. Is there an answer to it at all? Why not rest content with the fact that this is the way it happened and so be it? But does not this simple connection between stars and me, a self-reflective being, drive me, not content with simple factual connections, to ponder an answer?

There are, of course, ready answers available to a religious believer. But the question really challenges those of us who, while respecting religious belief, know its limits. We wander in the universe and seek to understand within the landscape we travel, that of the universe itself, how we have come to be and how we have come to ask such questions. Since the questions arise from necessary connections that we find in the universe itself, e.g., stars and us, we seek the answers also there. But we are almost inevitably drawn into the mystery of it all and to ask the question, Why? Could intelligent beings come to

be, had there been no stars? Would we even be here to
ask such questions, had there been no stars?

Stars Tell Us Where We Are

Stars are also the means whereby we can measure distances in the universe and, therefore, locate where we
are. As the earth goes about the sun each year, we note
from the opposite ends of that orbit, i.e., at intervals of
one-half year, a shift in the apparent position of nearby
stars against an unshifting background of very distant
galaxies. The nearby stars have, of course, a larger shift
and the distant ones a smaller shift until the very distant
galaxies have no shift at all. Thus we determine the distance of nearby stars relative to our distance from the sun
about which we orbit by measuring this angular shift, the
parallax angle. But this technique allows us to measure
distances only to some hundreds of light years, a short
distance indeed in the universe, since we know that the
nucleus of our galaxy is thirty thousand light years distant and the nearest galaxy to us about 2 million light
years away. The most distant galaxies seen are billions of
light years away.

How are we able to measure such large distances? We
begin to develop ways in which we can use the brightness
of stars as a measure of distance. Since the brightness
of any point source varies inversely as the square of the
distance from us, if we know the real brightness we can
measure its distance by measuring how bright it appears
to us. It happens that, among the stars for which we can
measure parallax, there are pulsating stars whose bright-

ness varies in a very periodic manner as they alternately get bigger and cooler and then smaller and hotter with each pulsation. Furthermore, the period with which they pulsate is very closely related to their intrinsic brightness, so that by measuring their period of light variation and their mean apparent brightness, we can determine how far away they are. In this way by identifying such stars in our own galaxy and in nearby galaxies, we were able to measure distances. In this way we were able to locate our position in the galaxy and the position of our galaxy in the nearby universe.

To measure larger distances, we must find even more energetic stars, such as supernovae, and eventually even entire galaxies whose intrinsic brightness we can estimate, which means that we can also estimate their distances relative to brighter nearby objects. Finally for very distant objects we use the expansion rate of the universe itself as a measure of their distances.

It is important to note that all distance measurements rely for their accuracy upon the standard distances measured by parallax. We should also note that the error in measuring distances increases with distance, since we are making increasingly broader assumptions as to the intrinsic energy output of certain standard objects and eventually about the expansion of the universe.

In addition, therefore, to being the source of the chemicals that make our bodies, stars are the beacons which tell us where we are in the universe. But we must be able to interpret the light coming to us from those beacons and intercompare the different kinds of beacons. We must also be cautious, as we measure larger and larger distances, to acknowledge the increasing uncertainties. Yes, stars are the beacons to tell us where we are in the universe; but we must admit that we are always struggling, especially as we look at the very distant universe, to know our place.

Families of Stars

It is interesting to note that stars, for the most part, are born into families. A single massive cloud of gas and dust breaks up and fragments of various masses collapse to form stars of various brightnesses and temperatures. While the more massive stars form more rapidly than the less massive ones, the time required for the birth of a star is much shorter than its total lifetime. The sun, for instance, was born, as we have noted, in one five-hundredth of its lifetime, five times faster than that for a human being. Thus, we may without exaggeration refer to a family of stars, just as we refer to the ensemble of the children born of the same parents.

A cluster of stars, born of the same molecular cloud, form in this sense a family of stars. They are bound together by a shared force of gravity about a common center of mass. They share a common place in the universe, and, until they eventually disperse, they move together through the universe. They are very much like a human family of one generation which lives together tightly for a period of time. As it matures it disperses when the children pursue independent careers, and it eventually disintegrates as a family. It is also true that, like human families, there are successive generations of stars, each succeeding one related to the previous. In fact, as we have seen, it is this succession of generations that provides the chemical elements for the origin of biotic systems, ourselves included, in the universe.

In reflecting upon this analog of star clusters to human families, we note a structural element in the universe, let us call it "family," which repeats itself at different levels: planets, stars, galaxies, etc., and that this structure perdures through the physical to the organic to the biotic universe.

Within these families of stars, there are often smaller units of multiple stars and many binary stars. Since stars in general are very distant relative to the dimensions of things in our everyday lives — telescopes, cars, houses, ourselves, the earth itself — it is impossible, except in a very few cases, to actually see two stars. How, therefore, do we come to detect that a single point of light is actually a binary star?

There are essentially two ways of detection, both of which require that the orbital plane of the two stars as they move about their common center of mass is not very tilted to our line of sight. Because of this requirement, many binary stars remain undetected. If this requirement is met, then with sophisticated instruments we can detect the motions of the stars toward us and away from us as they move about in their orbits or we can detect the diminution of light as one star passes in front of its companion and eclipses it. In some cases we can detect both phenomena.

These are few and very precious cases, because they provide us with the most detailed information possible for determining the masses of stars. If we can detect both eclipses and orbital motions then we can reconstruct the true orbit of the stars about their common center of mass and we can then use Newton's law of gravity to calculate the masses of the stars. We have already seen that a knowledge of the masses of stars is fundamental to knowing how they are born, live, and die. And since we have been born of stardust, in studying these stars we are studying our own beginnings.

Telescopes and the People with Long Eyes

We should note that, in order to understand a star, we had to intercept its light with large, sophisticated telescopes and analyze that light with complicated instruments, such as those which allow us to classify stellar spectra. We were thus extending our knowledge, as we have noted above, to objects that were trillions of times further away than the extent of our outstretched arms.

Even the sophisticated instruments that astronomers use may be thought of as part of ourselves. A story is told of Native Americans in Arizona, the Tohono O'Odham, at the time that the United States government was considering the building of a national astronomical observatory at the top of a mountain which was part of their reservation and was sacred to them. The government and the tribal council entered into treaty agreements, but it soon became clear that there was no word for astronomer in the Indian language. Although they spent their lives under the beautiful starry skies of that part of the world, they did not study the stars as astronomers do.

So in order to prepare written agreements the Indians invented a word in their language which upon translation means "The People with Long Eyes." Their insight is a very significant one. The instruments and techniques that astronomers invent are a part of themselves; they are an extension of our curiosity to know. We have come to know the stars by being people with long eyes, and what we have discovered is that we have come from the stars.

Is there, from what we have discussed above, a "social" character diffused throughout the universe: "families" of galaxies, of stars, of planets, of nations, of people? And is there not evidence of a common bond among these "families"? We have already seen that the more abundant chemical elements in our own bodies came from three generations of stars and that some of the less abundant elements may have required nucleosynthesis in millions of distant galaxies. While as scientists we are still groping to understand this apparent "social" character of the universe, we are already convinced that no element in the universe, including ourselves, can be ultimately understood, except in relation to the whole.

When Galileo first targeted the universe with his telescope, he saw myriads of stars like our sun, but they were at distances no greater than about ten thousand light years. When the Hubble Space Telescope, after its original optical problems were corrected, observed the universe, it saw clusters of galaxies at about 8 billion light years distance, about one-half of the way back to the Big Bang. Most recently nodules of gas, dust, and young stars at somewhat larger distances have been observed. There is some indication that they may be primordial galaxies. If so, this will be the first observational evidence we will have of how galaxies are formed. As our eyes get longer, the mysteries of the universe continue to unfold before us. The following chapter will show how.

Chapter Eight

A MYRIAD
OF ISLAND UNIVERSES

T HE ANCIENT GREEKS, and also the great civilizations which preceded them, could not but be impressed when, upon lifting their eyes on high to the heavens on those clear, dark nights which they fortunately enjoyed, they saw a belt of light girdling the sky. They came to call it the Milky Way, thinking that it was the milk of Juno. But they had not the slightest idea that this could be an independent system of stars.

From Our Galaxy to the Extragalactic Universe

It was only, in fact, in 1785 that William Herschel established that the Milky Way was actually explained by the fact that the solar system was part of a much larger grouping of stars which we were viewing from our place within it. And it was only about fifty years later in 1840 that we came to know of the spiral structure of what at that time were called nebulae and which were thought to be stellar groupings within our Milky Way. We then began to suspect that even our Milky Way might have such a spiral structure. The first problem to be attacked, however, was to classify those extended and nebulous objects which showed a spiral structure.

At the beginning of the twentieth century the astronomer Vesto Melvin Slipher made an important observation. The spectrum of the Andromeda nebula showed spectral lines which were displaced due to the Doppler effect. He then also observed that twenty-five other nebulae had Doppler shifts, some toward the red and others toward the blue. Slipher interpreted these shifts as due to the movement of the source, the nebulae, toward or away from the observer, and he concluded that the Milky Way was itself a great spiral nebula which contained the solar system moving within the nebula which, as the other nebulae, was also moving in the universe. The movement of the center of the universe from the earth to the sun may have seemed spectacular. But this was truly amazing. The whole solar system was moving within a nebula, the Milky Way, which itself was moving with other nebulae in the universe.

These conclusions were the result of observations, but they also came about only after a celebrated public debate between two of the chief astronomer protagonists of that time, Harlow Shapley and Heber Curtis. This debate became important not only because of the ideas which surfaced there but more importantly because it concretized the way in which scientific knowledge was to be acquired. Ideas and hypotheses may not always be correct, but open discussion of them could lead to further understanding if one respected the provisory nature of the results. Such an attitude should be characteristic not only of the scientist but of anyone who is truly searching for the truth. From his data Shapley concluded that the sun was not at the center of the galaxy and that the galaxy was much larger than had been thought. Curtis argued that the spiral nebulae were external galaxies and that the Milky Way was one among many galaxies, called "island universes." Each of the protagonists had reasonable arguments. The discovery in 1917 of three novae each in a different spiral nebula gave further support to the extragalactic nature of the respective spiral nebulae.

A definitive answer, however, came only with the discovery by Edwin Hubble of a Cepheid variable star whose light varied with a period of three days in the Andromeda nebula. By then it was well known that the brighter Cepheids had longer periods. The brightness of Hubble's Cepheid determined from its period was such that it had to be, according to the determinations available at that time, at the enormous distance of at least 1 million light years and, therefore, clearly outside of our Milky Way. The fact that individual stars could be seen in the Andromeda nebula had its own importance. Hubble soon discovered other variable stars and novae.

And so the universe continued to take on a new image. It was much larger than anyone had imagined. The idea of an infinite universe, already considered by some medieval scholars, no longer seemed so far fetched. Discoveries such as that of Hubble were moving the frontiers to ever more distant horizons.

Still many details remained to be explored. What were the real dimensions of the Andromeda nebula? What was its true distance? Further advances in technology were required, and these came about with the construction of the great telescope at Palomar. Observations of Andromeda confirmed that it was a galaxy, slightly larger than the Milky Way and at a distance of about 2 million light years. Walter Baade, observing with the Palomar telescope, came to these conclusions.

We would do well at this time to dwell for a moment upon the influence of technology, such as the development of the Palomar telescope, on scientific discoveries. In so doing one could give the impression of being preoccupied with the wish to reassert the superior role of the human being with respect to mere technology. We recall from the previous chapter how an indigenous people of the Arizona desert, the Tohono O'Odham, described astronomers as "The People with Long Eyes." In their unique way they saw the telescopes which astronomers used in their research not simply as instruments made of glass and metal, but as extensions of themselves. Telescopes were the long eyes of the astronomer. This is an excellent example of how we might view the technology that serves us to understand the universe and ourselves as part of it. Technology provides us the possibility to go beyond our natural limitations by using our intelligence to bring the resources of the natural world into our adventurous passage through the universe.

The discovery of Andromeda as a galaxy like our own Milky Way led the way to a whole new view of the universe and ourselves in it. At the same time as Baade was being led to his discovery, Hubble was in the process of calculating that the age of the universe was about 4 billion years. But this was obviously in conflict with the estimation by geologists for the age of the earth. And there was another observation that began to worry scientists. Urbain-Jean-Joseph Le Verrier had discovered in 1859 that the perihelion of Mercury was changing its position in an anomalous way. It was becoming increasingly clear that this could not be squared with Newton's law of gravity.

The Trembling Pillars of Knowledge: Something New on the Horizon

The magnificence of James Maxwell's theory of electromagnetism remains without precedent. He had unified what was known of radiation, of electricity, and of magnetism. Still there was the growing uneasiness, first grasped by the physicist Hendrik Lorentz, as to whether electromagnetism might have something to do with the very nature of space and time. And how was one to confront Albert Michelson's claim that electromagnetic waves required a ghostly "ether," which no one could detect?

And so the theories of both Newton and Maxwell were being challenged. It appeared that something new would be required to explain a universe that was becoming ever more grandiose and full of mysteries. Once again a tension was growing between different ways of viewing reality, a healthy tension which promised to help us grow in knowledge. As one might expect, that is exactly what happened.

A young physicist, Albert Einstein, appeared on the scene and unified the tensions so brilliantly that his name is synonymous with the theory he discovered. The

problems raised by Michelson's experiments were solved
by Einstein's special theory of relativity, while the intuition of Lorentz was brought to a happy conclusion with
the general theory of relativity. Einstein's general relativity presented a completely new way of viewing the
relationship between matter, space, and time. It was essentially a completely new view of gravity, but it was
untested. It soon met the challenge by explaining the
precession of the perihelion of Mercury. The observation of a star, although it was physically occulted by the
sun, provided another test of the theory, in this case the
interaction between matter and electromagnetic waves.

General relativity added a new dimension to the universe. We could no longer think of the universe as
imbedded in a three-dimensional space but rather had
to view it as being in a continuum of four-dimensional
space-time. But the most important result was that this
new theory proposed to be able to investigate the universe
as a whole. The harmony of the universe, sought with
such difficulty over so long a period of time, seemed to be
at our fingertips. The laws and numbers of general relativity would explain it all. The struggle of human thought
to unveil the secrets of nature was being rewarded by a
physical-mathematical theory. Once again the universe
could be considered a "cosmos," but now somewhat
differently than had been understood in ancient times.

As one approached the very early moments of the universe even the theory of relativity was insufficient, and it
was necessary to apply quantum mechanics, which studies and describes the world of the infinitely small. We had
on the stage, therefore, at this point two theories, one

for the macrocosm and the other for the microcosm. But were these two compatible and, if so, how? This question does not yet have an answer despite the efforts of the world's best physicists. Modern research is going to the limits to see if it is possible to develop a quantum theory of gravitation, that is, a theory which would successfully reconcile the two worlds, that of the infinitely large and that of the infinitely small. Many problems arise, however, about how to interpret the results of quantum mechanics.

These problems, such as the role of the observer in the process of measuring and the dependence of the measurement itself upon the measuring technique and the object being measured, bear upon epistemology. It is not clear how the action of the observer affects the measurement. The effect of the observer could be very important because in addition to the indeterminacy principle, which says that in the microscopic world we deal in probabilities, it would place serious limits on our capacity to understand nature, at least that kind of understanding determined by the rules of classical physics. Most contemporary scientists are seriously concerned about the consequences. In fact, in the microscopic world the concept of probability reigns in such wise that for a particle of a given energy we can only say that it has the maximum probability to be located in a given position, but that probability is always less than one.

Since we wish to come to know the very first moments in the evolution of the universe, we must push our investigations to the moments when the universe was very small, so small that it is necessary to consider the universe itself as a microscopic particle with all of the quantum uncertainties we have just discussed. And so at this point the various interpretations of quantum mechanics play a direct role in the history of the universe and our understanding of it. We find ourselves confronted by an obstacle which seriously challenges our ability to understand the physical reality of the universe. We have no intention of waxing mystical. However, it is difficult to avoid the conclusion that there is something in nature itself which colors our search for knowledge by empirical measurements with wonder and amazement. This experience of the unknowable could become a stimulus to take up new paths in our efforts to understand the universe and ourselves in it.

An Expanding Universe

We now return to the work of Hubble. Having established the reality of the "island universes," as he called them, the task was now to come to a more complete understanding of their recessional velocities. The answer was provided by Hubble relying upon the contributions of Carl Witz. Hubble tried to find a relationship between the distances and radial velocities of the galaxies. He found that the distance increased linearly with the radial velocity. This became known as the Hubble law, and the constant of proportionality between the two parameters became known as the Hubble constant. With certain assumptions it became the constant which was used to determine the age of the universe. But was the Hubble law valid everywhere and at all times? The observations of clusters of galaxies carried the law to very large distances, and, in fact, the measured radial velocities allowed one to determine the distances from the Hubble law.

There remains an underlying problem, not altogether settled yet, about the interpretation to be given to the observed red shifts. If they were truly due to Doppler shifts, then, since all extragalactic objects showed the shift, the interpretation was that the entire universe was expanding. This same interpretation resulted from the solution of Einstein's equations, and, in fact, Einstein refused to accept this solution and he arbitrarily introduced a constant which canceled out the expansion.

It appears that even great minds at times succumb to preconceptions, as in this case did Einstein. Still he had the wisdom to recognize his mistake, and some years later he corrected his theory. Science was not at the root of the preconception. There was a prejudicial idea that a static universe was to be preferred to a dynamic one. Traces of this prejudice remain for those scholars who find it difficult to accept that the red shifts measured for quasars are really cosmological. This is only one example of the fact that scientific research is not extraneous to criteria which are more esthetic than scientific. In this case science could have become stalemated by such preconceptions, were it not for those who had the courage and the inclination to reconsider their own preconceived certainties. Only when one accepts the risks involved in reviewing one's positions, hopefully on a scientific basis, will progress be made in our scientific understanding.

If, indeed, the universe is expanding, then there comes spontaneously to mind the idea that at one time the universe was more condensed. To put it in another way, in the past galaxies must have been much closer together. At some time, they must have even been piled up so densely that as time shrunk to the initial moment, time zero, there was no space. This was truly a revolutionary idea. An expanding universe might imply that it had a beginning, and now it was physics that was suggesting this premise, a premise that is called the singularity. Not all physicists, however, are inclined to admit the existence of such a singularity. It is not only physics which causes some hesitation. Some would be tempted to see in this singularity the instant at which creation occurred, the *fiat lux* of the Bible, which gave origin to everything. They would, therefore, implicitly claim to find precisely in this singularity a proof of God's existence and the metaphysical origin of all that exists.

It is obvious that we have here two different ways of viewing the singularity: the physical meaning arising from a scientific interpretation of the expanding universe and the religious meaning of the relationship between faith in a creator God and the physical reality of nature. This latter is a very delicate matter and can easily lead to solutions which smack of either scientism or fideism. Nonetheless, the matter is, in our opinion, a real one and cannot be done away with in a facile manner. Science should not be subordinated to faith nor faith to science; nor should either be excluded. To us these extreme positions do not adequately accept the specific differences in the two approaches to reality, two approaches which are more correctly seen as deriving from different experiences of one and the same reality.

We insist upon this notion of human experience because it brings into consideration not only the fact of measurement but also the more comprehensive task of the human person to reflect upon and interpret the measurements made. Only in this way do the measurement and its meaning become appropriated personally and thus have the capacity to bring the experimenter not only to a deeper knowledge but also to true wisdom. To put it in another way, we believe that reality speaks more eloquently to one who approaches it with different languages and with different things to say. True understanding requires that we not exclude any language or expressions. It is important, therefore, to know the various languages whereby reality speaks to us. Only thus will we come to the most comprehensive and deepest knowledge of all that exists. Rooted deep in this multidisciplinary way of approaching reality is, we propose, an attitude of humility and wonder as we face it all.

Let us go back to the discussion of the singularity. Stephen Hawking resolves the problem by essentially eliminating it. He proposes that there is no physical meaning to the singularity as such. The crucial issue is not whether his solution to the problem is the correct one or not. What is of capital importance is the approach to the problem. Once again we detect, even if only implicitly, a preconception which wishes to eliminate any trace of transcendence. It is as if one wished to prevent nature from speaking more eloquently and in a richer manner than a purely scientific approach would allow.

It may be true that from purely scientific considerations this is a legitimate and even necessary way of proceeding, that is, to eliminate transcendental considerations. It would be difficult to imagine a faith which is founded upon scientific proofs. Still we cannot help but see this exclusively scientific approach to reality as being an attempt to reduce the understanding of reality in all of its richness to science alone. Furthermore, even should the singularity be shown to be true or false, this is not, we propose, essential with respect to the expression of an act of faith in God the Creator, since that act is founded upon a personal encounter with God. Once again we detect an extreme simplicity hidden in every attempt to prove or disprove the existence of God from purely scientific considerations of nature.

At this point we can think of the age of the universe as the time that has intervened between that singularity, the beginning of time, and today. As such, that age is, with some assumptions, equal to the inverse of the Hubble constant. But, as we have already mentioned, this contrasts with the geological age of the earth. The earth would be older than the universe! Obviously, there was more work to be done. Yet again, it was not possible to say that we had arrived at the desired answers. Researchers were once again confronted with a conclusion which would entice them to seek out the truth. Their knowledge was incomplete, and they would have to submit the results thus far achieved to further critical analysis.

It soon became clear that the data used up until that time were seriously in error, particularly those which had been used to measure distances. When corrections were made, a more acceptable value for the Hubble constant was obtained, although it was certainly not viewed as definitive. No one, of course, thought the expansion would necessarily have been constant; in fact, it was more reasonable to think that it had been larger in the past than it is today. That implies that the Hubble constant varied with time and this would bring about a further increase in the age of the universe and make it even more compatible with geological age determinations of the earth.

A Universe of Great Variety

Once the reality of "island universes," galaxies outside our own, had been established, it became clear that there were a variety of galaxy types. Again it was Hubble who proposed a classification of them. But what was the real reason for the variety of forms? Was there some link between the various types of galaxies? One thing was clear: galaxies could be distinguished between those that were rich in gas and dust and those that had little. The former were spiral galaxies, the latter ellipticals. Now the presence of gas and dust is important for the formation of new stars, since this occurs precisely where gas and dust are abundant. This gas and dust may be enriched by the explosion of supernovae, stars which explode at the end of their lives and supply heavier elements, the fruit of thermonuclear synthesis, to the interstellar medium. Elliptical galaxies are less disposed toward star formation since they have little gas and dust and thus contain mostly old stars. Spirals have both old and young stars.

Together with the development of technology, refined

ways of observing have been developed in the last thirty years. Thus new windows on the universe have been opened up and have brought to light many new and unexpected findings. Others, indeed, were predicted by theory. Radio signals were detected, and it was precisely the observation of a radio source at the moment of its occultation by the moon that allowed Martin Ryle to identify it with a blue star-like object of magnitude thirteen. Maarten Schmidt obtained a spectrum of this object with the Palomar telescope and discovered to his surprise that superimposed on the continuum there were emission lines which could not be identified with any known element.

Schmidt's intuition was remarkable. He hypothesized that what was actually being seen were hydrogen lines red shifted by the Doppler effect by an amount never seen before. If his intuitions were correct, then the universe would be even larger than had been suspected up until then. And, if this were true, then such distant objects would have to have enormous intrinsic energies in order to be visible. But what mechanism could produce such immense energies? Soon thereafter many other similar objects were discovered, and they were called "quasars," for quasi stellar objects, since they had the appearance of a stellar image in telescopic observations. Several thousands of such objects have now been discovered. It soon became clear that these objects had other peculiarities. Some of them showed brightness variations. Some were compact and emitted x-rays, gamma rays, and infrared radiation.

General relativity predicted the existence of ultracompact objects which could cause a curvature of space in their neighborhood so great that it would obstruct the emission of electromagnetic waves from their surface. These are the famous black holes, which swallow up any form of material close to them and thus give rise to the emission of immense amounts of energy. Up to the present the only imaginable energy source for quasars appears to be supermassive black holes.

Characteristics similar to those of quasars were observed in other extragalactic objects such as Seyfert galaxies and BL Lacertae objects. The similarities among these objects led to the introduction of a new category of extragalactic objects called AGNs, for active galactic nuclei. Later on the discovery that some quasars are surrounded by nebulous material and show absorption lines further advanced the view that these objects had something in common.

We would still like to know whether there is any relationship between AGNs and normal galaxies. Did they have different origins or are we witnessing different stages in the evolution of galaxies? These are still open questions to which we have only partial answers. One fact is clear: we see quasars only out to a certain distance, beyond which, at least with current instruments, we see no more of them. Why this cutoff?

The First Awakenings

At the beginning of the 1960s two engineers at the Bell Telephone Laboratories in New Jersey discovered a strange phenomenon as they were testing a new antenna for satellite telecommunications. They could not remove a certain background static. This static turned out to be a signal which was coming from all directions in the sky and corresponded to an emitting source at a temperature of three degrees Kelvin. Strangest of all, the source appeared to be the whole sky itself. For some years before that several models of the universe were being studied, and there was one which seemed to be a favorite. It was referred to as the "Big Bang," a name invented by Fred Hoyle, an opponent of the model. This model predicted that there would have been a residual radiation from the time when the universe was very hot and that it would be equal in all directions and at a temperature of three degrees Kelvin, having cooled down as a result of the expansion of the universe.

Robert Dicke and Jim Peebles at Princeton, also in New Jersey, were at that time the chief proponents of the Big Bang model. A lunchtime conversation among the four soon brought together the observations and the theory, and the cosmic background radiation was discovered. It was an important and critical result. It is interesting to us because it adds a fundamental item to the catalogue of objects in the universe, an item which permeates and envelopes everything and whose origins can be traced to times even more remote than those of the most distant quasars. If the universe is about 15 billion years old, this radiation would come from a time about three hundred thousand years after the Big Bang. Once again the intelligent interplay and dialogue between observations and theory had led to a discovery so fundamental that cosmology would never be the same.

And so the universe is much richer in its contents than one could have imagined at the beginning of the twentieth century. But there is still more. Estimates of the mass of the universe from the movement of objects within it give values quite a bit larger than the sum of the masses of all visible objects. Thus a large part of the mass of the universe, counting radiation in all spectral bands, cannot be seen, at least with instruments currently available to us. Up to now the nature of this invisible mass is unknown, although many candidates have been proposed but must still be verified.

It seems that every time we try to understand some further secret of the universe, it sets itself to remind us of our ignorance and of the tentative nature of what we know. The universe, it seems, is prepared to yield up its secrets when we are prepared to admit that we are limited and that we are wayfarers. Should this not be the posture of researchers as they meet nature? Are we confronting something which is mechanically determined or so determinable once and for all? In such a case we could foresee the end of science when all of the laws which govern the universe become known. Or are we before something whose seemingly interminable richness excites us and causes us to marvel and to wonder? To marvel is the trait of one who like a child knows how to rejoice and to take pleasure in even the smallest of novelties. But it is also the trait of the wise old person who knows how to taste every one of life's fragments, however small and insignificant it may appear to be. It is this sense of marvel which tickles the curiosity to raise always new questions and which permits one to look upon the obstacles which arise, as one searches for wisdom, as only temporary.

If one is dealing with such objects as clusters of galaxies or extremely compact objects, the law which governs the universe as we know it is that of general relativity. The curvature of space time, predicted by general relativity, is weighty in these cases where we have enormous concentrations of mass in galaxies and clusters of galaxies. In fact, we have in these cases powerful gravitational lenses which not only create many images of the same visible object which lies beyond them, but also make visible objects which would not otherwise be detected because they are either too distant or are hidden by the very foreground mass which is lensing them. On the other hand, for less massive concentrations Newtonian gravity still works.

Models of the Universe

If we sum up all of the galaxies to the visible horizon of the universe, we arrive at some tens, if not hundreds, of billions. However, the mean distance between galaxies is so great that, should we spread out all of the mass uniformly, we would have a near vacuum with a mean density of about one atom per cubic centimeter. This is an important result when we come to speak of the future of the universe, since it is precisely the density of matter which will determine that future.

We have now come to the point of discussing, at least in a summary fashion, those models of the universe which, among today's researchers, appear to be the most likely or are at least the most discussed. We have already spoken of one of the great steps forward in our understanding of the universe when in ancient Greece a geometrical model of the world was first proposed. The importance of this step lay in the fact that for the first time one sensed the possibility of being able to reduce vast and complicated processes to a limited and relatively certain number of laws which governed the relationships between them. This would make possible a description of natural phenomena in a kind of universal, comprehensive, and synthetic language. And so we come to a discussion of the various models which are proposed to describe the universe and which are written in the language of mathematics.

As we have already seen the observed red shift of galaxies, clusters of galaxies, and quasars is an indication of the fact that the universe is not static but rather expanding. This, of course, assumes that the red shifts are cosmological. An expanding universe is further supported by the discovery of the three degree cosmic background radiation, which points to an epoch when the universe was much more concentrated than it is today. From these considerations we are naturally drawn to ask whether it might be possible, at least ideally, to go even farther back to a time when the universe was even smaller and even to the moment of the Big Bang. Such an adventure is not an easy one for at least two reasons. As we approach the moment of the Big Bang the changes in the newborn universe follow upon one another at a heady pace as one important stage succeeds another, each of them very short and each with its own specific physics. Second, there are intrinsic limits to the observability and measurability of these processes. Quantum mechanics imposes precise limits on what we can and cannot observe and measure. The indeterminacy principle of Heisenberg, of which we have already spoken, takes command when we try to investigate regions with dimensions smaller than 10^{-33} centimeters. (See the appendix [p. 173] for a description of the successive stages in the evolving universe.)

Two problems arise from the description of this model: the flatness and the homogeneity of the universe. How did it ever come about that the universe has almost no curvature? And how did it ever happen that the cosmic background radiation is so homogeneous after 15 billion years? An attempt to answer these questions was proposed by Alan Guth in 1980 when he suggested that there was an inflationary epoch in the expanding universe between $t = 10^{-35}$ and $t = 10^{-24}$ seconds after the Big Bang. According to this hypothesis an extremely small part of the newborn universe would have expanded in every direction at superluminal velocities so that the universe which we see today would simply be the result of this expansion of a little bubble. The extremely small dimensions of the original bubble would have allowed the bubble to expand homogeneously in all successive stages of the expanding universe. Furthermore, given the very small dimensions of the bubble, the universe which came from it would appear very flat, just like our universe. This appeared to be an ingenious solution, although recent data, which indicate that the universe may actually be accelerating in its expansion, seem to put everything back on the table for discussion.

We should recall at this point an obvious but important fact: the velocity of light is finite. In view of this, let us reflect upon inflationary models of the universe, whereby the universe inflated at velocities much greater than the velocity of light. If our observable universe has come about by the inflation of a small bubble in the original universe, it is quite likely that there are other such universes, originating from other bubbles, with which we cannot communicate because they are at distances larger than light could travel in the total time since the inflationary epoch. Thus, our attempt to understand the whole universe is futile. We can only know about a small, inflated bubble of it. While, therefore, the inflationary models may explain the flatness and homogeneity of our universe, they leave us in the sad state of never being able to know the ultimate and profound secrets of the whole universe. Yet once again we find ourselves facing a barrier. What attitude should we take? Do we surrender to the inevitable or do we courageously seek alternative scientific explanations? Do we rest content in untouchable certainties or do we, without regret, seek for other paths of discovery? At any rate, we must never tire in our daily journey in the search of truth.

In the 1970s an additional hypothesis was put forth, namely, that there was a stage during the Planck era when the four fundamental forces were united into one force. With the expansion and cooling down of the universe each force at a specific epoch separated out. Gravity was the first to separate, and this happened at the end of the Planck era at a temperature of about 10^{32} degrees Kelvin. The weak nuclear force then separated out at the beginning of the inflationary epoch at a temperature of about 10^{27} degrees Kelvin. The strong nuclear force and the electromagnetic force would have separated out about 10^{-12} seconds after the Big Bang at a temperature of about 10^{15} degrees Kelvin.

Many questions are still unanswered or only partially answered within the general framework of this model. How did matter aggregate to form galaxies, clusters of galaxies, and superclusters? Does the distribution of matter which we see today in the universe reflect something of the original distribution? Could the very weak differences detected in directions in the cosmic background radiation eventually explain the inhomogeneities from which the current distribution of matter was generated? In which sequence were galaxies, clusters of galaxies, and superclusters formed? From the larger to the smaller or the smaller to the larger aggregates? In whichever direction this would have happened, gravity played the central role.

One of the characteristics of science is that it is able to make hypotheses about the future of the phenomena it studies based upon the laws of nature. To hypothesize about the future of the universe is an unusual activity since the universe is unique. It has no equals. There is nothing with which to compare it. Everything depends upon the mean density of the universe. If it exceeds a critical value, expansion will stop at a certain point and an accelerating implosion would begin driving the universe to collapse back to a cosmic singularity. If the density is less than the critical value, the universe is open and will expand forever, star formation will cease, and we will finally have a universe in which galaxies would contain only white dwarfs, neutron stars, and black holes at about 10^{12} years after the Big Bang. At about 10^{27} years galaxies themselves would be transformed into black holes of galactic dimensions, and after about 10^{31} years the galactic black holes would aggregate to form supergalactic black holes. The stellar black holes would evaporate in 10^{67} years, the galactic ones in 10^{97} years, and the supergalactic ones in 10^{106} years. With every evaporation of a black hole there would be an emission of energy. And everything would finish in a final absolute darkness in the most unimaginable cold or heat.

Our View of the Universe Is Changing

As we think upon what we have just discussed, the profound difference between present-day models of the universe and those of our ancestors becomes quite clear. We see especially how the initial points of view were so different. For our ancestors the universe was the stage where the divine powers played out their desires; their view was theological and teleological. For us the universe is governed by strict physical laws expressed in mathematics, laws which are part of the universe itself and are not the result of the whims and fancies of the gods. This change in point of view is an enormous leap, and it drives us to ask some fundamental questions about both the way we are thinking and what we are thinking.

In fact, these assertions of modern cosmology seem like metaphysics, a pursuit hardly suitable to the methods of scientific enquiry, which require the reproducibility of experimental data. Furthermore, we could raise the question as to whether cosmology is a science at all since the object under investigation is unique and it is not possible to perform reproducible laboratory experiments on it. It is not that we wish either to deny or to affirm a metaphysical nature of the laws of mathematical physics. It is simply that the kind of language that makes an absolute denial of certain affirmations is by necessity metaphysical, especially when one is dealing with matters which concern the presuppositions of science rather than science itself.

Many attempts have been made to provide a purely physical-mathematical description of the world, and these efforts continue. Apart from their success what they truly reveal is a kind of fundamental drive, especially among scientific researchers, to unify and synthesize. The so-called theories of everything are a good example of this tendency, at least when they attempt to bring together in a single analysis the whole universe, including the human being and all the experiences which make one precisely human. Fortunately not all such theories make such wide-sweeping claims. For instance, John Barrow at the beginning of his book *Theory of Everything* says:

> Of course, we must be circumspect in our use of such a loaded term as "Everything." Does it really mean everything: the works of Shakespeare, the Taj Mahal, the Mona Lisa? No, it doesn't. And the way in which such particulars of the world fit into the general scheme of things we shall discuss at some length in the pages to come. It is a vital distinction that needs to be made in our approach to the study of Nature. For we might like to know if there

are things which cannot be straitjacketed into the mathematically determined world of science. We shall see that there are, and we will attempt to explain how they may be distinguished from the codifiable and predictable ingredients of the scientific world that will populate any Theory of Everything.

The description of the universe which we have just seen lends itself to reflections such as these, especially when one has come to realize that the physical universe is ruled by phenomena which are bound to the constants of nature, a circumstance which has led some to see a kind of purpose intrinsic to the history of the universe. But such reflections drive us on to others such as the very nature of the laws of nature, the predilection of nature to mathematical formulations, the existence or not of specific initial conditions for the universe, and, not least of all, the role of the human in the history of the universe.

At the end of these final steps taken in our wanderings in the universe, steps which have driven us toward frontiers which we could not even have imagined fifty years ago, it might be helpful to look back at the path we have taken. Although we will speak more about it in the next chapter, we are driven here to open our thoughts to the marvel that reaches to the heart of the matter as we realize that we are returning home, to the earth and to the human spirit. Looking back on where we have been, we could either be overcome with terror or we could be in ecstasy as we come to realize what we have found: a universe of such immense richness, variety, complexity, and grandeur, and then to know that it is where we have been born.

To be aware of this in one fell swoop is surely a supremely human act, maybe unique in the history of the universe. We have thus come to discover that reflections on the universe are truly reflections about ourselves. So, in a real sense the universe speaks to us, or, more to the point, it speaks about us. All the more should we marvel and rejoice! Such joy, born of knowing, is really an expression of love, a participation in that "love which moves everything," to use Dante's expression. If the believing person truly accepts what the Scriptures in Psalm 19 state:

> The heavens declare the glory of God,
> And the firmament proclaims his handiwork (19:2),

it is perhaps not an exaggeration to paraphrase this verse and apply it to us humans and claim that the heavens speak of us and declare our grandeur. In fact, the Psalmist himself in Psalm 8 states:

> If I look at the heavens, the work of your hands
> The moon and the stars which you have set there,
> What is man that you remember him,
> The son of man that you care for him?
> And yet you have made him just a little less than the
>   angels,
> And with glory and honor you have crowned him,
> You have given him power over the works of your hands,
> You have placed everything under his feet. (8:4–7)

For the one who pursues science as a believer, we propose that these expressions of the Psalmist are less an established fact than they are an indication of the path to be taken and of the method to be applied in the constant and continuous search not only for knowledge but for wisdom.

~ Chapter Nine ~

JOURNEY
WITHOUT END

W E HUMAN BEINGS are a part of a universe; in its evolution we have come from it; we are evolving with it, and we have the capacity to think about it. But today science itself seems to be pushing us beyond the knowledge of the universe and ourselves, to something that is more than knowing.

In us the universe can reflect upon itself. Evolution is no longer, if ever it was, a blind, unconscious, and un-comprehending process. In us the evolving universe has become a voyage. At times there are forced marches, at times refreshing pauses to reflect; we meander in our search to understand the universe and ourselves in it, but we have a tenacity, and, although we are always con-scious of our ignorance, we sense that we have an ever more refined sense of what we do not know. The aware-ness of our ignorance draws us forward in an ever more passionate desire to understand. And yet there seems to be more to it than understanding. We have an un-easy feeling that we may never really fully understand, that our voyage will never end. But this does not cause us to despair. It rather spurs us to wonder why this is so. Why are we drawn ever onward, searching for an understanding of it all but never reaching the ALL?

The Many Ways of Knowing

To understand has many meanings. There are many ways to seek understanding. As we have seen, the development of the natural sciences in the sixteenth and seventeenth centuries has had an enormous success in helping us to come to an understanding of the universe and ourselves in it. Mathematics and physics have provided us with precise and exacting methods to penetrate the mysteries of the universe. They have had amazing success, and yet they inevitably bring us face to face with the inexplicable: to understand light we must think of it as both a particle and a wave; we cannot know exactly both the position and the motion of a particle of matter; i.e., there is an intrinsic indeterminacy in the universe; two persons traveling at different speeds will age at different rates. These and other paradoxes are inevitably involved in our attempt to understand the universe through physics and mathematics.

The natural sciences are, of course, not the only way to come to an understanding of the universe and ourselves. There are literature, history, the social sciences, philosophy, theology, etc. But the natural sciences have had and continue to have a dominant influence on our thought. One reason for this is certainly the great success that they have had both in our knowledge and in the technical applications deriving from that knowledge. But another, perhaps more important, reason is that they continuously open up for us the marvels of the universe. From the intricate patterns of DNA to the magnificent structure of galaxies we are brought to wonder: to wonder about origins, to wonder about ends, to wonder about purpose, and, yes, to wonder whether involved in it all there is a person.

Questions without Answers

Questions are raised by the natural sciences which do not appear to be answerable by the rigorous methodology of the natural sciences. Why, for instance, does the universe seem to be so fine-tuned to life? This question has been discussed by cosmologists over the past two decades as the "anthropic principle in cosmology." Many distinctions are made concerning its true meaning; they range from the so-called "weak" principle, which essentially states that, as observers in the universe, we see the universe as related to us, to the "strong" principle, which requires a certain teleology intrinsic to the universe. For our purposes it is necessary to state only the following well-established cosmological facts: (1) the existence of the human being has required a fine-tuning of the physical constants and the laws of nature which we find empirically by scientific investigation in the universe; (2) there is no general cosmological theory which explains why those constants should have the precise values they do and the laws should be as they are.

Many examples of the fine-tuning we have referred to have been discussed. The argument is essentially the following one: of the many constants of nature, e.g., the velocity of expansion of the universe, the mass and charge of the electron as compared to the proton, the gravity constant, etc., the empirically measured value is so precise that had it been only slightly different (in general, one part in one million) it would have been impossible for human beings to have emerged. Why, therefore, are the values of all the constants so precisely what they are?

Let us look at just a few examples. In expanding since its beginning in a Big Bang, the universe has cooled to the current temperature of about three degrees Kelvin. In so doing it has followed the normal, well-known law for gases: as a given volume of gas collapses it heats up; as it expands it cools down. If the current temperature of the universe were much different than it is, the earth would not be able to dissipate its energy and it would continuously heat up. Life on the surface of the earth would not be possible beyond a certain temperature. Why is it that the temperature of the universe is just the value that it is, after having begun at millions of degrees? Examples of this kind could be multiplied many times over. For instance, if the energy levels in helium, carbon, and nitrogen were not precisely the values they are, the thermonuclear fusion processes which have given us the heavier elements could not have taken place. Without those heavier elements we would not be here.

In fact, in order to have the right proportion of elements in the universe to form the human organism, three generations of stars were required. The only way known to scientists to manufacture the heavier elements is in the thermonuclear furnaces of stars. As a star lives out its life it converts the lighter elements (hydrogen, helium, etc.) into the heavier elements (carbon, silicon, oxygen, etc.). When it dies, it regurgitates this heavier material to the universe. The next generation of stars, born from this material, goes through the same life cycle, so that the universe is being constantly supplied with the heavier elements. To arrive at the chemical abundances required for the human organism three generations of stars had to perform in this way.

So our chemical origins are in the stars and we are intimately related to the energy and the matter in the universe of which we are a part. We are constantly exchanging atoms with the total reservoir of atoms in the universe. Each year 98 percent of the atoms in our bodies are renewed. Each time we breath we take in billions and billions of atoms recycled by the rest of breathing organisms during the past few weeks. Nothing in my genes was present a year ago. It is all new, regenerated from the available energy and matter in the universe. My skin is renewed each month and my liver each six weeks. In brief, human beings are among the most recycled beings in the universe.

The cosmologist, of course, first seeks the answer to the anthropic principle in a general physical theory that will explain all of the values. No such theory yet exists. Next, we seek to explain the fine-tuning by statistics. Pure chance is ruled out because the probability that it could have happened by chance is unacceptable scientifically. The statistical argument then moves to the possibility that there are many universes, existing either simultaneously or successively. Each of these universes would have its own set of physical constants and of the laws of nature. If we have enough such universes, even an infinite number, then the probability that one such universe like ours would come to be is quite acceptable. However, none of these many-universe proposals succeeds very well, either because data are lacking or they are not verifiable. Verifiability is an important and indispensable criterion of scientific validity. In the many-simultaneous-universes theory the universes are separated by distances greater than the light travel time for the total age of the universe and, therefore, in principle nonverifiable because noncommunicating. In the successive-universes hypothesis it is difficult to see how there could be any possible data which could verify the existence of a universe before the last Big Bang.

Is there a life-directedness in the universe? Did the universe have a beginning? Will it have an end? All such questions inevitably draw us beyond the natural sciences to the philosophical and religious implications of the results derived from the natural sciences and the questions left unanswered. And yet we must resist the ever recurring temptation to drag in the so-called "God of the gaps" to attempt to supply for our own ignorance in the natural sciences by some theological or philosophical construct which we have no rational grounds to supply. The passion to understand must not be allowed to drive us to an unwarranted confusion between scientific knowledge and religious knowledge or, for that matter, any other kind of knowledge.

On the other hand an honest evaluation of conclusions reached by the natural sciences may serve as an invitation to think transcendentally. Beauty, as we have seen, is one of the criteria by which we judge the content of a scientific theory. But the beautiful reveals itself to us in many ways: through the symmetry, simplicity, and universality of a mathematical theorem; through the smile of Mona Lisa; through the banded colors of a rainbow. The beauty in any one of these is not exhausted by nor completely captured by any of the others. The beauty of Mona Lisa's smile cannot be explained by mathematical formulas; the beauty of a rainbow is not exhausted by an analysis of the refraction and reflection of light waves in water droplets. Among the criteria, therefore, for judging the truth value of the results from any of the disciplines we have mentioned we must list its unifying explanatory power.

The Biblical View of God and of the Universe

In the beginning chapters we discussed the primitive reflections of our ancestors upon the nature of the world about them and its intimate relationship to their gods. At this final stage of a more mature reflection upon the scientific venture, let us amplify our reflection upon the Genesis account of creation as one example of how the beginning and the end of our voyage have much in common with respect to the unification of our experience as wanderers in the universe in search of meaning.

It is important to note at this point how the biblical account of creation in the book of Genesis highlights the comment made by God after each act of creation: "And he saw that it was good." The Hebrew word used to express "good" has, in fact, a strong indication of something esthetically pleasing, so that, without betraying the original, one might translate the comment: "And he saw that it was beautiful." Thus, every creative act of God becomes a source of beauty, and, as a sharing in God's creation, every human creation, the invention of a new scientific theory, for instance, is a source of beauty.

A study of the Old Testament shows that the first reflection of the Jewish people was that the universe was the source of their praise of the Lord who had freed them from bondage and had chosen them as his people. The Psalms, written for the most part well before Genesis, bear witness to this: "The mountains and valleys skip with joy to praise the Lord"; "The heavens reveal the glory of the Lord and the firmament proclaims his handiwork." But if these creatures of the universe were to praise the Lord, they must be good and beautiful. Upon reflecting on their goodness and beauty, God's chosen people came to realize that these creatures must come from God. And so we have the stories in Genesis in which at the end of each day God declares that what he had created is good (beautiful). The stories of Genesis are, therefore, more about God than they are about the universe and its beginning.

The authors of Genesis are not, in the first place, speaking of the origins of the created world. They are speaking of the beauty of the created world and the source of that beauty, God. The universe sings God's praises because it is beautiful; it is beautiful because God made it. In these simple affirmations we may trace the roots of modern science in the West. The beauty of the universe invites us to know more about it, and this search for knowledge discovers a rationality innate in the universe.

There are two implicit assertions in Genesis which set the faith of these people apart from their predecessors, the Canaanites, upon whose stories they rely. First, God is one and there is no other god; there is no struggle between God and some equal, even malevolent force. Second, everything else is not God, but depends for its beauty upon him. He made everything and declared it beautiful. It is very important to note that created things are first of all beautiful because God says that they are; it is only upon reflection in a second moment that they are seen as understandable, as having a rational structure. By its very nature beauty is inexhaustible and cannot be neatly packaged. The beautiful can be enjoyed only by one who does not attempt to cage it in or make of it an exclusively private possession. Beauty is for all and cannot be privatized. It cannot be quantified. It dies under any rationalistic attempt to measure it. It is for this reason that, as this closing chapter's title indicates, the goal is forever drawing us forward in what we sense as an interminable journey to understand. Beauty is irresistible; beauty draws us to seek understanding.

The Unification of Our Knowledge

For instance, the inability to provide thus far a strictly scientific explanation to what is a strictly scientific problem, i.e., the anthropic principle, as we have just discussed, may be, according to the discussion above of the criterion of unifying explanatory power, an invitation to consider that the explanation lies in a teleological consideration. It is important here to emphasis the word "invitation," so as to preserve the epistemological independence of the various disciplines. One is perfectly free to accept the invitation or not. One can stay firmly put within one's own discipline and continue to seek the answer there, uncontaminated by possible solutions arising elsewhere. But it seems to us that the invitation is a very real one and well founded; it, therefore, also seems to us that it requires serious reasons to reject it. Those serious reasons must confront the long history of philosophical and theological thought that holds that there is a person at the source of the existence of the universe and that said person had a purpose or a design in "creating" the universe, a design which included, perhaps even centered upon, our existence.

The criterion of unification of our knowledge appears to extend the epistemological nature of the natural sciences toward the realm of other disciplines, such as philosophy and theology. Put in very simple terms this criterion is nothing else than a call for the unification of our knowledge. One could hardly be opposed to that. The problem arises with the application of this criterion. When is the unification not truly unifying but rather an adulteration of knowledge obtained by one discipline with the presuppositions inherent in another discipline? History is full of examples of such adulterations. It is for this reason that scientists have always hesitated to make use of this criterion. And yet, if applied cautiously, it appears to us to be a most creative one for the advancement of our knowledge.

The supposition is that there is a universal basis for our understanding, and, since that basis cannot be self-contradictory, the understanding we have from one discipline should complement that which we have from all other disciplines. One is most faithful to one's own discipline, be it the natural sciences, the social sciences, philosophy, literature, theology, etc., if one accepts this universal basis. This means in practice that, while remaining faithful to the strict truth criteria of one's own discipline, we are open to accept the truth value of the conclusions of other disciplines. And this acceptance must not only be passive, in the sense that we do not deny those conclusions, but also active, in the sense that we integrate those conclusions into the conclusions derived from our own proper discipline. This, of course, does not mean that there will be no conflict, even contradictions, between conclusions reached by various disciplines. But if one truly accepts the universal basis we have spoken of above, then those conflicts and contradictions must be seen as temporary and apparent. They themselves can serve as a spur to further knowledge, since the attempt to resolve the differences will undoubtedly bring us to a richer unified understanding.

The above discussion particularly applies when we are addressing fundamental and ultimate questions in cosmology. How did the universe begin? Is the universe finite in space, in time? Is our intelligent civilization unique in the universe? Does the existence of intelligent beings in the universe have a significance for understanding the universe as a whole? Does our knowledge of God depend on our understanding of the universe? In fact, a very strong piece of evidence that there is a universal basis for understanding is the very clear drive of the human being for meaning. This is seen clearly from the very dawn of human history where, with even a very primitive collection of data, our ancestors sought meaning in the physical universe, as well as in the events of their personal lives and those of society in general.

There are many risks involved in the attempt to unify our knowledge. Physical cosmologists speak today of the "Theory of Everything" and of knowing the "mind of God." The search for a "Theory of Everything" is an attempt to find a unified theory which will include all known fundamental forces. It is essentially an attempt to find the ideal mathematical structure which is at the source of all created reality. Indeed, experimental results, for instance, the discovery within the past years of a new quark, continue to urge on the quest. But one gets the distinct impression that the quest itself goes on in a very Platonic atmosphere of mathematical physics and that eventual empirical verification in our world of shadows is of secondary interest. It should be noted, however, that, in the tradition of Archimedes, the quest began with and is sustained by evolutionary cosmologies which have come forth from empirical quantitative measurements of essential parameters which characterize the universe, such as the time dependence of temperature and density in an evolving universe. In fact, it is thought that the unifying structure dates to a time very close to the Big Bang and that multiplicity came about by symmetry breaking as the universe cooled and became less dense.

This brings us back to questions about life in the universe. Whether life is unique to the earth in all the universe is insignificant to the following questions. Had we been given the initial physical parameters in an expanding universe at some time near the Big Bang (a few Planck times), could we have predicted that life would come to be? We assume that the honest quest for a unified theory means that we could have predicted the emergence and the exact nature and strength of the four fundamental forces and such fundamental physics as that. But is life the result of so many bifurcations in nonlinear thermodynamics that we could not have predicted, even if we possessed the Theory of Everything and knew all the laws of microscopic and macroscopic physics, that it would come to be? We are asking questions somewhat different from those raised by the anthropic principle, whether taken in the weak or strong sense. The questions there have to do with interpreting or explaining the fine tuning of all of the physical constants and conditions required for the emergence of life. We are asking whether, given antecedently all of the physical constants and conditions necessary for life from our *a posteriori* knowledge of it, could we have predicted that it would have come to be? Did life happen to be or, given the conditions for it, did it have to be?

The Mind of God

It is not unusual for cosmologists to speak of the "mind of God." In most cases, it appears, this is taken to mean that ideal Platonic mathematical structure from which the shadow world we live in came to be. If we were to understand that structure, we would have a unified theory and thus an understanding of all physical laws and the initial conditions under which they work. Would we also fundamentally understand life? There appears to be no intentionality associated with the "mind of God" of the new physics. Can life be understood without that intentionality? These are, we accept, pretentious questions which go beyond what a scientist would usually accept as a rational approach to the world in which we live.

When scientists in their enthusiasm speak about the "Theory of Everything" and the "mind of God," they inevitably try to quantify what is not quantifiable: selflessness, graciousness, harmony, etc. Musical scales can be carefully analyzed by mathematics; the beauty of a Mozart nocturne cannot. This is, of course, not to minimalize science, nor, as a matter of fact, any of the other ways of knowing. It is simply to realize what a given discipline can or cannot do. That is precisely why our knowledge must be unifying. There will, of course, always be a tension between science and theology because of the transcendental (beyond reason) character of the latter, but considering the somewhat Platonic quest for the "mind of God" in the new physics that very tension could be the source of a quite creative dialogue.

In our age, perhaps more than at any other time, the scientific view of the world has been the principal spur to a more unified view of the world. It has opened our minds to the vast richness of the universe which cannot be appropriated by any one discipline alone. Science invites us to that vision. It also cautions us not to absolutize scientific results. We must beware of a serious temptation of the cosmologists. Within their culture God is essentially, if not exclusively, seen as an explanation and not as a person. God is the ideal mathematical structure, the theory of everything. God is Mind. It must remain a firm tenet of the reflecting religious person that God is more than that and that God's revelation of himself in time is more than a communication of information. Even if we discover the "mind of God" we will not have necessarily found God. The very nature of our emergence in an evolving universe and our inability to comprehend it, even with all that we know from cosmology, may be an indication that in the universe God may be communicating much more than information to us. Through the limitations of science we might come to see the universe as a unique revelation of God, that God is Love.

If we are truly seeking a wholeness, a unification of our knowledge, then upon reflection we note a certain dynamism in our voyage to understand, a dynamism that draws us from knowledge, through the incompleteness of our knowledge, to wonder and then to love. We propose one final example of such dynamism which has its source in our scientific knowledge.

By Coincidence or Planned?

There are two very different processes which have occurred in the evolving universe over lengths of time that are sufficiently similar that it has been possible for the two events to be concurrent. If they had not been concurrent, and we shall see they need not have been, we would not be here. For a moment let us limit ourselves to the scientific knowledge of these two events. As we saw in chapter 7, we have a sound scientific knowledge of the birth, life, and death of stars. The rate depends upon the masses of the stars; the more massive stars age more rapidly. From this analysis we know that the sun is about 5 billion years old and that it will live for another 5 billion years before it begins to die.

From the first appearance of primitive life forms on the earth to the appearance of intelligent life there was a period of about 3 billion years. Why was this period not many times longer or many times shorter than the lifetime of the sun? The two processes are very different and, therefore, the determination of the time durations are, as best we know, quite independent. The life of the sun depends upon gravity, gas laws, thermonuclear reactions, etc. The development of intelligent beings relies upon chemistry and ultimately biology in an evolving universe where an interplay of chance and necessity do not allow a clear determination of time durations. Why is it that the evolution of human beings fits comfortably into the lifetime of the sun? It is, of course, obvious that the beginning, development, and sustenance of intelligent life are dependent upon the sun. But that is precisely the scientific knowledge that leads us to wonder. How is it that the time scales for two very different processes, the life of the sun and the existence of intelligent life, the second of which depends upon the first, are concurrent? For instance, the time required to develop intelligence could have been so much longer that the sun would have died before it could happen.

As scientists we are cautious in our ignorance. As self-reflective beings we cannot but wonder that we are here at all to wonder because of the, apparently fortuitous, co-incidence between two time durations. We are, of course, grateful. We cannot resist a sense of awe and thanks. We may even be led to love what we sense. Are we going beyond our knowledge as scientists? Very definitely, yes. Are we being led astray from our scientific knowledge? You the reader must decide. We the authors offer the following response.

The immense richness of the world revealed by the sciences from the microcosm to the macrocosm, the passionate, insatiable desire we have to understand it, the mysteries and the paradoxes that continuously arise in our search, the haunting sensation that our quest may never end, all of these experiences may be leading us to a source that transcends understanding and is most fittingly approached as Love. This Love is self-revealing in all aspects of creation and is drawing us not only, or even primarily, to understand, but rather to love in turn.

We have admittedly presented this notion of love rather abruptly, and so it would be well if we elucidated it a bit. This does not mean that we shall try to define love. In fact, we are convinced that it is indefinable. We rather choose to speak about it in terms of what we, as scientists and as wanderers in the universe, have already seen in our journey to understand the universe and ourselves in it.

We are reminded of the love that the English poets Elizabeth and Robert Browning shared and their attempt to express it. Robert wrote a poem to Elizabeth in which he says: "How do I love thee? Let me count the ways. I love thee to the length and breadth and depth of every day's most quiet needs.. . . " Note that there is no attempt on Robert's part to define what love is. He directly addresses the question of How? And his response is equally as direct: "to the length and breadth and depth of every day's most quiet needs." Love is expressed in a response to needs, that of the lover and that of the beloved. It is not an abstract, fleshless, philosophical concept. It is a felt reality. It is a response to a need, a mutual and shared need.

If we retrace our journey, we will note again a continuing tension between our insatiable desire to know and understand and the lingering conviction that our desire will never be satisfied. This is where our quest for understanding becomes a search for love. We find ourselves in need. Our search has become ever more personal, not in the sense that it cannot be shared, but rather in that it can no longer be reduced to an intellectual search. We share it, but it is a pang of emptiness that cannot be filled by all that we know or can hope to know. Like Robert Browning we now sense a longing, which grows out of "every day's most quiet need." Our journey is no longer just an intellectual quest, a search for answers.

At this point the story of the great St. Augustine of Hippo comes to mind. His life is a paradigm of the turn our journey has taken. In his *Confessions* Augustine writes:

> Truth! truth! How the very marrow of my soul within me yearned for it as they dinned it into my ears over and over again! To them it was no more than a name to be voiced or a word to be read in their libraries of huge books. But

> while my hunger was for you, for Truth itself, these were
> the dishes on which they served me up the sun and the
> moon, beautiful works of yours but still only your works,
> not you yourself.

Augustine's years of learning had served only to increase
his hunger, his need for love. "You were deeper than my
inmost understanding," says he, "and higher than the
topmost height that I could reach."

Furthermore, although this love is, as we have already
admitted, indefinable, it is nonetheless a firm and solid
reality. As Augustine puts it:

> My love of you Lord, is not some vague feeling; it is pos-
> itive and certain. Your word struck into my heart and
> from that moment I loved you. Besides this all about
> me, heaven and earth and all that they contain, proclaim
> that I should love you, and their message never ceases to
> sound in the ears of all humankind, so that there is no
> excuse for any not to love you.

There are two expressions of Augustine here which are
true of our experience of love. The experience was initiated by the other: "Your word struck into me heart...,"
and, while the experience is very personal, it is also
meant to be universal: "... sound in the ears of all
humankind." The experience of our journey to understand the universe and ourselves has been just that:
while we with our own intellectual powers initiated the
struggle to understand, in the end we were struck by
love. And our journey has been a shared one. All of hu-
manity has been invited to be part of it and in the end
all are invited to pass from understanding to love.

In each step of our journey we have sensed that lingering need to understand more than we had understood so far. But it is only here near the end that we sense that the need we have accumulated is an invitation to love. Again, Augustine provides the classical expression for this late-blooming love:

> I have learnt to love you late, Beauty at once so ancient and so new! I have learnt to love you late. You were within me, and I was in the world outside myself. I searched for you outside myself . . . and I fell upon the lovely things of your creation.

While it may seem strange to some that the scientific quest to understand the universe and ourselves in it has brought us to this point where the search for understanding has led to Love, we have seen ample indications that we can rest peacefully, even as scientists and if only momentarily, in the direction our journey has taken. Although not completed, it has brought us a sense of fulfillment, of joy, and of gratitude that we have the capacity to enjoy the beauty of the universe, a beauty made richer by our scientific knowledge of it.

APPENDIX

We might list the following stages in the expanding universe according to the standard model:

t_0:

The Big Bang.

t less than 10^{-43} seconds:

The radius of the universe is about 10^{-33} centimeters; below this radius quantum effects dominate over general relativity; the universe is in a chaotic state with a density greater than 10^{94} grams per cubic centimeter and a temperature greater than 10^{37} degrees Kelvin; our notions of space and time go to pieces.

t less than 10^{-23} seconds:

Epoch of the quark; no structured particles exist; the mean density is 10^{55} grams per cubic centimeter, and the temperature is about 10^{22} degrees Kelvin; the radius of the universe is about 10^{-13} centimeters, about the size of a proton.

t less than 10^{-4} seconds:

Epoch of the hadron (heavy subatomic particles); the electromagnetic and the weak and strong nuclear forces come into play; matter is more abundant than antimatter by one part in a billion; at the end of this stage there is an annihilation between matter and antimatter, except for the excess mentioned.

between t=10^{-4} and t=one second:

> Epoch of the lepton (light subatomic particles); the electromagnetic and weak nuclear forces are at play.

between t=one second and t=10^6 years:

> The radiation epoch; radiation is denser than matter; electrons no longer scatter photons, and the universe is transparent to radiation; temperature is about 10 billion degrees Kelvin; deuterium is formed from the fusion of protons and neutrons; between 10^5 and 10^6 years hydrogen is formed at a temperature of about 3,000 degrees Kelvin.

t=10^6 years:

> Mean density is one atom of hydrogen per cubic centimeter; no galaxies yet formed.

between t=10^6 and t=10^9 years:

> Mean density is 10^{-22} grams per cubic centimeter; temperature is greater than 3,000 degrees Kelvin; quasars and galaxies are forming.

t=10^9 years:

> Mean density is 100 atoms of hydrogen per cubic centimeter; the formation of galaxies.

Today:

> About 15 billion years since the Big Bang; mean density is one atom of hydrogen per cubic centimeter; there are 10^{80} particles in the universe; 10^9 photons and neutrinos for every proton or neutron.

BIBLIOGRAPHY

Barbour, I. *Religion in an Age of Science*. San Francisco: HarperSan-Francisco, 1990.

Barrow, J. D. *Theories of Everything*. Oxford: Clarendon Press, 1991.

Barrow, J. D., and F. J. Tipler. *The Anthropic Cosmological Principle*. Oxford: Clarendon Press, 1987.

Blackwell, R. J. *Galileo, Bellarmine and the Bible*. Notre Dame, Ind.: University of Notre Dame Press, 1991.

Buckley, M. J. *At the Origins of Modern Atheism*. New Haven: Yale University Press, 1987.

Clayton, P. *God and Contemporary Science*. Grand Rapids, Mich.: William B. Eerdmans, 1997.

Clifford, R. J. *Creation Accounts in the Ancient Near East and in the Bible*. Washington, D.C.: Catholic Biblical Association, 1994.

Cohen, I. B. *Isaac Newton's Papers and Letters on Natural Philosophy*. Cambridge, Mass.: Harvard University Press, 1958.

Corey, M. A. *God and the New Cosmology*. Lanham, Md.: Rowman & Littlefield, 1993.

Davies, P. *The Cosmic Blueprint*. New York: Simon and Schuster, 1988.

———. *God and the New Physics*. London: J. M. Dent and Sons, 1983.

———. *The Mind of God*. London: Simon and Schuster, 1992.

de Duve, C. *Vital Dust*. New York: Basic Books, 1995.

Dreyer, J. L. E. *Tycho Brahe*. New York: Dover Publications, 1963.

Dyson, F. *The Origins of Life*. Cambridge: Cambridge University Press, 1985.

Fantoli, A. *Galileo: For Copernicanism and for the Church*. 2d ed. Vatican City: Vatican Observatory Publications, 1996.

Eigen, M. *Steps towards Life*. Oxford: Oxford University Press, 1992.

Garcia-Rivera, A. *The Community of the Beautiful: A Theological Esthetics*. Collegeville, Minn.: Liturgical Press, 1999.

Gilkey, L. *Nature, Reality and the Sacred*. Minneapolis: Fortress Press, 1993.

Gleick, J. *Chaos: Making a New Science*. New York: Viking, 1987.

Grant, E. *Planets, Stars, and Orbs: The Medieval Cosmos, 1200–1687.* New York: Cambridge University Press, 1994.

Harrison, E. R. *Cosmology.* Cambridge: Cambridge University Press, 1989.

Haught, J. F. *Science and Religion: From Conflict to Conversation.* New York: Paulist Press, 1995.

Hawking, S. *A Brief History of Time.* New York: Bantam, 1988.

Hoskin, M., ed. *The Cambridge Illustrated History of Astronomy.* Cambridge: Cambridge University Press, 1997.

Kaufmann, W. J., and N. F. Comins. *Discovering the Universe.* 5th ed. New York: Freeman, 2000.

Kuhn, T. S. *The Structure of Scientific Revolutions.* Chicago: University of Chicago Press, 1970

Livio, M. *The Accelerating Universe: Infinite Expansion, the Cosmological Constant, and the Beauty of the Cosmos.* New York: Wiley, 2000.

Lockyer, N. J. *The Dawn of Astronomy: A Study of the Temple Worship and Mythology of the Ancient Egyptians.* Cambridge: Cambridge University Press, 1964.

Lucretius, T. *De rerum natura.* Trans. A. D. Winspear. New York: Harbor Press, 1956.

Monod, J. *Chance and Necessity.* London: Collins, 1972.

More, T. *Isaac Newton.* New York: Dover Publications, 1934.

Murphy, N. *Theology in an Age of Scientific Reasoning.* Ithaca, N.Y.: Cornell University Press, 1990.

Pannekoek, A. *A History of Astronomy.* New York: Interscience Publishers, 1961.

Peacocke, A. *Intimations of Reality.* Notre Dame, Ind.: University of Notre Dame Press, 1984.

———. *Theology for a Scientific Age.* Minneapolis: Fortress Press, 1993.

Pedersen, O. *The Book of Nature.* Vatican City: Vatican Observatory Publications, 1992.

Penrose, R. *The Emperor's New Mind.* Oxford: Oxford University Press, 1989.

Peters, T. *Science and Theology: The New Consonance.* Boulder, Colo.: Westview Press, 1998.

Polkinghorne, J. *The Faith of a Physicist.* Princeton, N.J.: Princeton University Press, 1994.

———. *Science and Creation.* Boston: New Science Library, 1988.

Prigogine, I. *From Being to Becoming: Time and Complexity in the Physical Sciences.* San Francisco: Freeman, 1980.

Prigogine, I., and I. Stengers. *Order Out of Chaos*. London: Heinemann, 1984.

Puddefoot, J. *God and the Mind Machine*. London: SPCK, 1996.

Rees, M. *Before the Beginning*. Reading, Mass.: Helix Books, 1997.

————. *Just Six Numbers: The Deep Forces That Shape the Universe*. New York: Basic Books (Perseus Group), 2000.

Richardson, W. M., and W. J. Wildman, eds. *Religion and Science: History, Method, Dialogue*. New York: Routledge, 1996.

Ronan, C. A. *Changing Views of the Universe*. New York: Macmillan, 1961.

Rosen, Edward. *Copernicus and His Successors*. London: Hambledon Press, 1995.

Russell, R. J., N. Murphy, and C. J. Isham, eds. *Quantum Cosmology and the Laws of Nature*. Vatican City: Vatican Observatory Publications, 1993.

Russell, R. J., N. Murphy, and A. R. Peacocke, eds. *Chaos and Complexity*. Vatican City: Vatican Observatory Publications, 1995.

Russell, R. J., W. R. Stoeger, and F. J. Ayala, eds. *Evolutionary and Molecular Biology*. Vatican City: Vatican Observatory Publications, 1998.

Russell, R. J., W. R. Stoeger, and G. V. Coyne, eds. *Physics, Philosophy and Theology*. Vatican City: Vatican Observatory Publications, 1988.

Shea, W. R. *The Magic of Numbers and Motion: The Scientific Career of René Descartes*. Canton, Mass.: Science History Publications, 1991.

Smolin, L. *The Life of the Cosmos*. Oxford: Oxford University Press, 1997.

Swerdlow, N. M., and O. Neugebauer. *Mathematical Astronomy in Copernicus's De Revolutionibus*. Heidelberg: Springer-Verlag, 1984.

Tanzella-Nitti, G. *Questions in Science and Religious Belief*. Tucson, Ariz.: Pachart Publishing House, 1992.

Thoren, V. E. *The Lord of Uraniborg*. New York: Cambridge University Press, 1990.

Ward, K. *Religion and Creation*. Oxford: Clarendon Press, 1996.

Weinberg, S. *The First Three Minutes*. New York: Basic Books, 1988.

Westfall, R. S. *Never at Rest: A Biography of Isaac Newton*. New York: Cambridge University Press, 1990.

Wilson, C. *Astronomy from Kepler to Newton*. London: Variorum Reprints, 1989.

Wilson, E. O. *Consilience: The Unity of Knowledge*. New York: Alfred A. Knopf, 1998.

INDEX